# Gospel Fear

The Heart Trembling at the Word of God
Evidences a Blessed Frame of Spirit

Jeremiah Burroughs

Monergism Books

Copyright © 2023

Gospel Fear, by Jeremiah Burroughs

Published by by Monergism Books
P.O. Box 491
West Linn Oregon 97068
www.monergism.com

All rights reserved.

No portion of this book may be reproduced in any form without written permission from the publisher or author, except as permitted by U.S. copyright law.

Print: ISBN: 978-0-9893131-4-8
ePub: ISBN: 978-1-961807-81-5

# Contents

| | | |
|---|---|---:|
| | To the Reader | IV |
| 1. | SERMON I | 1 |
| | And that Trembleth at My Word | |
| 2. | SERMON II | 20 |
| | What the True Sanctified Fear of God and His Word is. | |
| 3. | SERMON III | 34 |
| | A Broken, an Humble Heart | |
| 4. | SERMON IV | 50 |
| | But by Way of Application. | |
| 5. | SERMON V | 67 |
| | Use | |
| 6. | SERMON VI | 81 |
| | The Preciousness of a Tender Heart | |
| 7. | SERMON VII | 94 |
| | Because thine heart was tender | |

# To the Reader

These following sermons are the works of the esteemed preacher, Mr. Jeremiah Burroughs, who is now a shining figure in the upper world. However, those who have been taken out of this sorrowful world and carried to the highest heaven by glorious angels have no need for the praise of humans, as they enjoy the presence of the eternal God. Therefore, I will turn my attention to these exceptional sermons that are presented before you. In the first three, you will discover a profound and glorious truth, namely, that a heart that trembles at God's Word is highly valuable in God's sight. This truth is explained clearly, supported thoroughly, and eloquently and faithfully applied. By God's grace, it can greatly contribute to the inner and everlasting well-being of your precious and immortal soul.

Before we proceed, let me clarify the various meanings of the term "Word" as used in the Scriptures. Firstly, at times, "Word" refers to the entirety of the Scriptures, both the Old and New Testaments. Secondly, "Word" may signify our Lord Jesus Christ, who is the life and essence of the Scriptures (as stated in John 1:3). Thirdly, "Word" can refer to the commands found in the Scriptures (Hebrews 1:4). Fourthly, "Word" may denote the warnings and threats issued by God. Fifthly, "Word" can represent the precious promises of God, as mentioned in Psalm 119:49. We should remember and hold on to these promises, as God is faithful and does not forget, but it is our duty to remind Him by actively seeking the fulfillment of His promises. Finally, "Word" can also pertain to the holy prophecies scattered throughout the Scriptures, as indicated in Jude 14.

This multifaceted understanding of the Word led a renowned minister in Germany, Baldusgar, to declare, "Let the Word of the Lord come, let it come, and we will willingly submit to it even if we had hundreds of necks to place under its yoke."

The purpose of the esteemed author in this small work is to persuade and influence the reader to submit to the Word, to be guided by the Word, to value the Word, to store up the Word, and to live according to the Word in a manner that reflects the teachings of the Gospel. The Jewish Rabbis used to say that there are mountains of profitable knowledge hanging upon every letter of the Law. I can assure you that in the following discussion, you will discover heavenly insights abounding in all the key points that this blessed author presents for your serious contemplation in this concise treatise. Here, you have Homer's Iliad condensed into a nutshell, containing abundant valuable material within a small space.

It is said of Caesar that he cared more for his books than for his royal garments. When he had to cross waters to escape his enemies, he carried his books in his hands above the waters but lost his robes. However, what significance do Caesar's books hold compared to God's books or to this little book now placed in your hands? Surely, the Word of the Lord is extremely precious to all those gracious souls who have a conscientious fear and reverence for it. Luther said he could not live even in paradise without the Word, but with the Word, he could endure living in hell itself. The philosopher expressed gratitude for being born in a time of true philosophy. Oh, how fortunate are we who are born in an era when the Lord pours out His Spirit abundantly, not in drops as in the time of the Law, but as showers of His gifts and graces. This was clearly evident in the author of this following piece. He was not just a day-star but the sun of righteousness that rose upon the people who were once privileged to sit under the author's ministry. It is also a great part of this world's blessings that they continue to be enriched by his excellent works to this very day.

One cannot claim that anything divine belongs to them until it resides in their heart. I can call a bird or any object mine when I hold it in my hand, but I cannot say that God is mine until He resides in my heart, or that Christ is mine until He resides in my heart, or that the Spirit is mine until He resides in my heart, or that grace is mine until it resides in my heart, or that the Word is mine until it resides in my heart. "I have hidden your word in my heart," says David, "that I might not sin against You." Therefore, dear reader, it is of utmost importance for you to internalise the Word that is presented before your eyes in this piece. Ah, Christians, your hearts are never in a better state, a safer state, a sweeter state, a happier state, a more gospel-oriented state than when they are in a trembling state. Therefore, make this little work your delightful companion until your hearts are brought into such a blessed state, and so on.

Obj. But can't reprobates and devils tremble at the Word? Didn't Belshazzar tremble at the handwriting? Didn't Felix tremble at the Word preached by Paul? And isn't it said that even the devils believe and tremble?

Ans. Wicked individuals and devils may indeed tremble at the judgments pronounced in the Word, but they do not tremble at the offense committed against God's holy commandments as sincere Christians do. In Ezra 10:3, Shecaniah declared, "We have trespassed against our God; let us make a covenant with our God according to the counsel of my lord and of those who tremble at the commandments of God." They tremble upon realizing their sins exposed by the commandments, whereas before, they were hardened in their practices such as marrying with the Canaanites. However, we find no evidence of this response in Belshazzar, Felix, or the devils.

Secondly, I respond that the wicked tremble but never mend their ways. Pharaoh trembled but never changed. Saul trembled but never improved. Belshazzar trembled but never corrected his actions. Felix trembled but never made amends. Even the devils tremble but never mend their ways. On the contrary, Paul trembled and cried out, "Lord, what do you want me to do?" The jailer also trembled and asked, "Sirs, what must I do to be saved?"

Thirdly, the trembling of the wicked pushes them further away from God and their duties. We see this in the example of Saul, who, in his trembling state, sought a witch. However, when godly individuals experience trembling, their souls draw closer to God. Jehoshaphat feared and set himself to seek the Lord, proclaiming a fast throughout all Judah. Saints, amidst their holy tremblings, pursue God fervently, just as the people followed Saul's tremblings.

[4] Fourthly, the godly tremble and mourn; their trembling hearts are broken hearts, and their broken hearts are trembling hearts. They look upon sin and tremble, and they look upon sin and mourn. In Jeremiah 25:13,17, it is written, "But if you will not listen, my soul will weep in secret places for your pride; my eyes will weep bitterly and run down with tears." On the other hand, the wicked tremble, but their hearts remain as dry and hard as rocks, even harder than rocks. In Jeremiah 5:3, it is said, "They have made their faces harder than rock; they have refused to return." Pharaoh trembled, yet he remained hardened, and the devils tremble, yet they too are hardened. If a single penitent tear could purchase heaven, hell could not offer that one tear. Repentant tears are precious. As Gregory said, they are the fat of the sacrifice; as Basil said, they are the medicine of the soul; as Bernard said, they are the wine of angels. However, these tears can only be found among those chosen souls who have a conscientious fear of God's Word and who possess the tender hearts depicted in this little treatise. Indeed, there is no worse state of spirit to encounter on this side of hell than the one that leads a sinner to shed counterfeit tears, to despise God's forbearance, and to rebel against His mercy. Such was the case with that profane Arian who was executed at Harwich, as recounted by Mr. Greenham in a strange and remarkable account. This hellish heretic, for that is how those who denied Christ's divinity were regarded in those times, shed a few insincere tears shortly before his execution and asked if he could be saved by Christ. When someone told him that he would not perish if he genuinely repented, he responded with these words: "No, if your Christ is indeed so easily persuaded as you say, then I defy Him and do not care for Him." Oh, what a horrible blasphemy and desperate wickedness! For a person to draw themselves away from repentance by using the very cord of love that should have drawn them towards it. But—

Fifthly, and finally, the hearts of wicked individuals and devils only tremble in anticipation of punishment and the impending judgment. It is similar to how a criminal trembles before the judge, weighed down by the sense of their impending doom. However, a child of God trembles under the weight of God's goodness and kindness towards them. In Hosea 3:7, it is written, "They shall fear the Lord and his goodness" or, as some interpret it, "They shall fear the Lord because of his goodness." The Hebrew phrase "pavebunt ad Dominum" can be understood as "trembling, they shall make haste to Him" (similar to how startled doves hasten to their nests, as seen in Hosea 11:11). Just as holy tremblings and gladness can coexist (Psalm 2:11), and as holy fear and joy can coexist (as seen in the women who left Christ's tomb with fear and great joy in Matthew 28:8, a peculiar combination of two contrasting emotions often found in the purest hearts), so too can holy love and trembling coexist. When a child, filled with love for their father, perceives that they have caused offense or sorrow, they tremble, much like the poor woman in Mark 5:33, who approached Christ with trembling, fearing that she had offended Him, yet with a heart full of love for Him. Thus, when a child of God fixes one eye upon the holiness and justice of God, they tremble; and when, at the same time, they fix their other eye upon the patience, goodness, graciousness, and willingness of God to forgive as a father, they experience love and joy. However, the trembling of the wicked arises solely from the anticipation of impending wrath and the torment they already feel in their conscience, even before reaching hell. I thought it necessary to mention these five points so that the reader may be better equipped to address the same objection when encountering it in this small work.

The refreshing dew of heaven has abundantly fallen upon many, yet like Gideon's fleece, they remain dry while the regions around them are soaked. Isn't this the case with many nowadays, who sit under the preaching of the Gospel and have access to the works of renowned men every day? And yet, how is it that their souls resemble the mountains of Gilboa, upon which neither dew nor rain descended? This is truly a lamentable state. When the books of the law accidentally fall to the ground, the Jews immediately declare a fast. Oh, my friends, what reason do we have to fast and mourn when we witness the Word preached, printed, and offered being trampled upon today by atheists, papists, Socinians, and other vain individuals? The Jews have a law that commands them to pick up any piece of paper they find lying on the ground, lest perhaps the Word of God be written on it and unknowingly trodden underfoot. While

Christians should be free from such superstitious concerns, they ought to be extremely cautious that not even the smallest iota of the Word, the slightest truth revealed in the Word, be trampled underfoot by themselves or others. We must consider its excellence and usefulness as a guide, as a light that leads us through the wilderness of this world towards the heavenly Canaan. Proverbs 6:22 states, "When thou goest, it shall lead thee; when thou sleepest, it shall keep thee; and when thou awakest, it shall talk with thee." According to the gloss of the Rabbinical interpreters, this means that the Word will lead you in your journey through this world, it will keep you when you lie down in the grave, and it will speak to you when you awaken at the glorious resurrection. But to keep the introduction brief, I shall hasten to a conclusion. Among all others, there are three types of individuals to whom I earnestly recommend this treatise.

[1] Firstly, this treatise is intended for those who tremble at the Word and possess tender and sensitive hearts. They will discover valuable comforts, special encouragements, and exceptional support to uplift and sustain them during their greatest trials, whether internal or external, and even in the most challenging of times.

[2] Secondly, it is also meant for those who are bold sinners, secure sinners, insensitive sinners, and unaware sinners. They will encounter a variety of arguments that aim to awaken, startle, soften, and bring them into a state of trembling and tenderness. The treatise provides them with specific guidance and advice on how to attain those spiritual dispositions that hold infinitely more value than all the crowns and kingdoms that people are presently striving for at the cost of bloodshed.

[3] Thirdly, it is intended for those who experience numerous fears, doubts, and internal debates regarding whether they truly tremble at the Word and possess a tender heart. I dare to assert that such individuals will find in this treatise those blessed truths that, through divine blessings, will dispel their fears, resolve their doubts, and bring a favorable resolution to all their internal struggles.

Reader, once you have sincerely read through this small treatise, I am confident that you will readily agree with me on the following points: Firstly, the two main themes discussed here, namely, our trembling at God's Word and possessing a tender heart, are of great significance and weight. Secondly, they are noble and essential aspects that all should strive to understand and comprehend in order to attain blessings in this life and happiness in the hereafter. Thirdly, they are timely and appropriate subjects for the days and times in which we live, characterized by a multitude of sins and accompanied by severe spiritual judgments such as blindness, hardness, and insensitivity. Fourthly, these themes encompass various other crucial points that are intricately intertwined and dependent upon them. Lastly, they are not frequently addressed from the pulpit or widely disseminated through printed materials.

Reader, a dear friend has convinced me to trouble you with reading this letter. Now, I shall conclude with a few words of advice.

1. Let the person who lays their eyes upon this book not borrow it, but purchase it.

2. Read it with seriousness.

3. Value it greatly.

4. Pray earnestly over it.

5. Strive to align both your heart and your life with the teachings found within it.

6. Treasure it among your most prized possessions.

7. And when you are in a position of spiritual strength, remember the sincere and heartfelt desire of the writer, reader, and listener that this little piece may be greatly blessed.

With that, I bid you farewell and rest,
Your true friend and servant to your soul,
Thomas Brooks.

# Chapter One

# SERMON I

## And that Trembleth at My Word

—And that trembleth at my Word. -Isaiah. 66.2.

The intention of the Holy Spirit, at the beginning of this chapter, is to redirect the people's hearts away from finding satisfaction in the magnificent temple they possess and the outward acts of worship they engage in. The Holy Spirit accomplishes this through two arguments presented at the start of the chapter. Thus says the Lord: "Heaven is my throne, and the earth is my footstool. What significance does it hold, then, that you have built such a glorious temple for my honor? I have no need for it, for my throne is in heaven, and the entire earth serves as my footstool. So where is the house you have built for me? Where is the place of my rest?"

Furthermore, not only does God have His throne in heaven and the earth as His footstool, but He has also created all these things. He reminds them that He is the one who has made the entire world. They may consider the temple they have built as something grand, but in reality, God has created the entire world, and if He so desired, He could have made a thousand more worlds.

As for outward acts of worship, God wants to discourage them from finding satisfaction in these alone. Therefore, He informs them that when they rely on outward duties while living wickedly, it holds no more value to Him than the slaying of a man. He expresses His abhorrence through four illustrations: First, killing an ox is akin to killing a man. Second, sacrificing a lamb is like cutting off a dog's neck. Third, offering an oblation is akin to offering swine's blood. Fourth, burning incense is comparable to blessing an idol. These are strong expressions that reveal God's intense disapproval of outward services when accompanied by a sinful life. He provides the reason behind His stance—they have chosen their own way. As long as they persist in their own paths, their actions, no matter what they may be, are detestable in God's eyes. He will not regard their temple or their sacrifices.

So, what pleases God then? He answers this question in the second verse: "But to this man will I look, even to him that is poor and of a contrite spirit, and trembles at my word." It is as if God is saying, "Regarding your magnificent temple and all your sacrifices, what do they mean when you choose your own ways?" God looks upon those who are humble, contrite in spirit, and tremble at His word. The glorious temple and all the sacrifices cannot compare to the value of a heart that submits to God and reveres His word.

But are there any impoverished souls, any contrite hearts who acknowledge their own sinful nature? Are there any broken-hearted sinners among you who tremble at my Word? This means more to me than all the sacrifices you can offer. Here we have three qualifications of someone whom God will pay attention to and consider: one who is poor, has a contrite spirit, and trembles at my Word. Such an individual is the one I look upon, delight in dwelling with, and take pleasure in. Firstly, it is a poor spirit, then a contrite one, and finally, the one who trembles at God's Word. It is the third qualification that I wish to focus on: trembling at God's Word.

People of the world live extravagantly and possess cheerful spirits. As it says in Malachi 3:15, "And now we call the arrogant blessed." Your bold, joyful, and proud spirits are highly esteemed in the eyes of the world. However, if you want to know who is precious in God's eyes, it is the one with a poor, contrite spirit who trembles at the Word, those whom men despise. Who faces greater contempt from others than those with poor and contrite spirits whose hearts shake and tremble at God's Word? The bold and cheerful spirits of the world scorn being troubled by the Word. But God asks, "Is there anyone who trembles at my Word?" In a gathering as large as this, He searches through all to find if there is any impoverished soul who trembles at His Word. Such an individual is an object of special consideration to God.

May there be many such individuals in this congregation, even today, for God is looking among you. Oh, that He may find objects to gaze upon, those who are delightful in His eyes! And such individuals are those who tremble at His Word. Therefore, the doctrine we are to focus on is this:

Doctrine: A heart trembling at God's Word is highly esteemed in God's eyes.

To him I will look. Some translate it as "To that thing will I look." Oh, that's the thing I truly love to gaze upon—a heart that trembles in response to my Word. In the eyes of God, all the beautiful objects in the world are not as lovely as a heart that trembles at the Word. The Lord considers nothing in the world worthy of His gaze in comparison to this object. He looks upon it with great delight. He does not say, "To him will I look who does my Word, who obeys my Word," but rather "to him who trembles at my Word." As someone commented on this passage, there is often more godliness in the trembling of the heart than in the work of the hand. Many things may hinder a true, gracious heart from carrying out God's Word. The heart may genuinely receive the Word and desire to do it, but various obstacles may arise between the heart and the action, hindering someone with a sincere heart from fulfilling it. However, as long as there is a trembling frame of heart in response to the Word, that is what God looks at. Physicians may consider trembling of the heart as a disease, but this trembling of the heart is the excellence of the heart and the joy of the soul wherever it is found.

In 2 Kings 22:19, we see the example of Josiah, a king who merely heard the Word of God being read, and his heart immediately began to tremble. His heart melted before the Lord. Oh, what a blessing it would be for kingdoms to have their kings possess such tender hearts! If God were to grant the great leaders of the world such tender hearts that tremble in the presence of God upon reading or hearing anything from His Word, it would be a great mercy. It is fitting for the greatest individuals in the world to tremble whenever they encounter the Word of God.

Now, in addressing this point, there are four things that need to be done.

Firstly, briefly show how the heart is affected when it trembles at God's Word—what it means to have a trembling heart in response to God's Word.

Secondly, explore what a gracious heart sees in God's Word that causes it to tremble.

Thirdly, distinguish between the trembling of a gracious heart and the trembling that may exist in a hypocrite. We find that even Felix himself trembled, and Scripture tells us that even the devils tremble.

Fourthly, the reason why God accepts such a heart, why it is so pleasing to God and why He looks upon it. These are the four aspects that need to be presented in the point, and they will lead to the application. The point is of great significance.

> First, such a heart holds high, honourable, and reverent thoughts of God's Word, even if previously it was lightly esteemed. The Word of God was considered no different from other words, like passing wind. But now the soul holds very high, honourable, and reverent thoughts of the Word of God, with a profound appreciation for it. It regards the Word with solemn thoughts, realizing that it is indeed its very life.
>
> Secondly, as a result, the soul attentively listens when the Word is either read or preached, regardless of how it is delivered. It eagerly attends to it and sets its heart upon it. As Moses said to the people in Deuteronomy 32:46, "Set your hearts to all the words which I testify among you this day, which you shall command your children to observe to do, all the words of this law." Why? Because it is not a worthless or empty thing for you;

it is your life. Before, a person may have approached hearing the Word in an ordinary manner, simply to pass the time or to hear what someone had to say. But now, when God works this gracious frame in the heart, the soul sets itself to it as to its life, recognizing that it is not a worthless thing.

I see that my life is in it, and there is a reverent attention to the Word of God. Fear causes the eye to be fixed. When someone has a fearful apprehension of something, it causes their gaze to be fixed upon it. Similarly, when there are many among the audience who tremble at God's Word, it captivates their attention. Their thoughts are directed towards it in a solemn manner, and they dare not allow themselves to be distracted, not even with wandering thoughts or looking around. They are attentive, eager to hear what God has to say to them.

Thirdly, when such a person has heard the Word, they do not dare to dispute against it. It is true that one may examine the preached word, but not to dispute against it. Prior to attaining this trembling frame, the heart may be prone to rise against the Word and entertain objections and futile arguments. However, now that the heart trembles at it, it does not dare to cavil and object as it did before.

Fourthly, the heart that trembles at the Word considers it a dreadful condition to have the Word speak against them. It regards it as the greatest evil for the Word of God to be against them, to hear it speaking against them and proclaiming threats. Oh, this is an uneasy state! How can I eat, drink, or sleep peacefully when the Word of God is against me?

Fifthly, a heart that trembles at the Word receives every command of the Word with reverence and humility. It submits itself to the Word and does not resist any part of it, neither the commands nor the threats. It opens itself to receive and embrace whatever the Lord has to give. There was a saying of someone who declared, "Let the Word of the Lord come, and we will submit even if we had six hundred necks to place beneath it." Similarly, a heart that trembles at the Word does not resist it but willingly opens itself to receive everything the Lord has to offer.

Sixthly, even the promises in God's Word are received with trembling. This means that the heart apprehends the immense distance between God and itself, as well as its own unworthiness of the mercy extended through the promise. Though the heart takes hold of the promise, it does so with reverence and fear. Therefore, a heart that trembles in this manner at the Word of God is precious in God's eyes and receives His attention.

Now, what is it that a gracious heart sees in God's Word that causes it to tremble? Understanding this will help you sanctify the name of God in many sermons to come. What God requires of all of you is that when His Word is sent among you, your hearts should not swell against it. Instead, you should receive it with a trembling frame of heart. Oh, the honour that would come to God and the benefit to your own souls if you were to receive it with a trembling frame of heart! I will show you the reasons why a gracious heart has cause to tremble at God's Word, what it sees in it. It is not out of weakness of spirit that it does so, but the Lord reveals it in His Word to the heart, leaving it no other option. In Judges 3:20, when Ehud came to Eglon, the King of Moab (a pagan king), he prefaced his message by saying, "I have a message from God for you." Notice how the king responded, he immediately rose from his seat in reverence for the Word that came from God. You should regard all the ministers of God who reveal His truths to you with great reverence. God cannot but take offense when He sees that even the most wicked person behaves irreverently towards his master, yet does not care about showing irreverence towards the Word of God. In Jeremiah 13:15, it says, "Hear and give ear; be not proud, for the Lord has spoken." If it is the Word of God, there must be no swelling of the heart against it. The greatest and most wicked pride of all is when people's hearts swell against the Word. Many of you may think that pride lies in clothing and appearance, but the greatest pride is when you rise against the Word. Many of you may think that there is no pride in your hearts, but how have you behaved when the Word of God has confronted your deepest corruptions?

First, it is the Word of God. He sees God in it.

Secondly, not only does he see that it is God's, but he sees an abundance of glory, majesty, greatness, and excellence of God that shines in His Word. The Lord reveals to this heart that there is an immense divine radiance and glory in the Word that it trembles at, which causes it to tremble. Among all things in the world, the Word of God contains the highest amount of God's glory. Though it is true that a soul, while in darkness, may not see any of this for a long time, when God's time comes to work graciously upon the heart, God opens up to this heart a divine radiance shining in the Word that it has never seen before. This makes the heart stand in awe of it more than ever before. In Psalm 138:2, it says, "For you have magnified your word above all your name." Or, as some read it more fully according to the original text, "You have magnified your word above all your name; that is, the name of God is magnified above all things. Oh, the Word of God contains more of God's name than the whole world! Take heaven and earth, the entire creation combined, and they do not possess as much of the name of God as the Word of God does. There is more of God, a greater and more divine radiance in the Word of God than in heaven and earth.

And therefore, by the way, you may be convinced of a great deal of ignorance and darkness that has been in you all this while. If we believe this truth that in God's Word there is more divine radiance than in all the creatures in heaven and earth, surely you have been in the dark. I appeal to your consciences: have you seen this divine radiance? We know that there is much of the glory of God in all His works - in the heavens, the sun, the moon, the stars. We behold the glory of God shining there. And in the seas, those who go down into the depths behold the wonders of the Lord. Even on the earth, all creatures cry out to us to fear the Lord and to tremble before Him. It is an indication of a stubborn, wretched, vile, and hardened heart that does not tremble before the Lord as He appears glorious in His great works. Every creature cries out to us, "Oh, will you not fear the God who has made me?" Every creature calls out, even though you may have had a deaf ear until now, it calls out, "Will you not fear the God who has made me?" Yes, God Himself wonders that mankind does not fear Him upon considering the glory that shines in some pieces of His work. In Jeremiah 5:22, God asks, "Fear you not me?" Will you not tremble at my presence? God speaks in a way of admiration. He wonders that men have such hard hearts. "What? Will you not fear me, who has placed the sand as the bound of the sea by a perpetual decree, so that it cannot pass it? And though its waves toss themselves, they cannot prevail; though they roar, they cannot pass over it." God only mentions this one work of His. Oh, is there any bold, desperate sinner who will not fear such a God as I am, who does such a great work as this? And then again, in verse 24, the Lord mentions another work of His. God wonders that men do not say in their hearts, "Oh, let us fear God who gives rain! We see that we depend upon the God who gives rain. Oh, therefore let us fear Him." Now God expects that all His creatures who see this glorious work should reason in this way: "Oh, what a glorious God is this, at whose mercy we lie! Let us fear this God!"

Well then, if God wonders that men do not fear Him upon seeing His glory in these two works of His, then He may wonder even more that men do not fear Him in light of all those glorious names of His that appear in His Word. Now, a gracious heart begins to see this, which it did not see before, and therefore trembles at His Word.

Thirdly, it sees more. It sees not only a divine radiance, but also a most dreadful authority in the Word of God. It is not just the greatness, splendour, and glory that causes fear, but the authority. If we were to see a prince in his greatness, in his pomp, it would cause some fear. But when we consider the authority that he has over us, that is what truly instils fear. In Jeremiah 10:6-7, it says, "There is none like you, O Lord; you are great, and your name is great in might. Who would not fear you, O King of the nations? For to you it appertains," etc. See how fear is grounded upon authority. "O Lord, you have absolute and supreme authority over all nations of the world. Who would not fear you?" Certainly, this is the reason why people's hearts are so vain and indifferent before the Word of God, because they do not apprehend the dreadful authority within it. It has authority that encompasses potentates as well as the poorest individuals living on the face of the earth. It has authority over all other authorities. It has authority over the heart, over the soul. Nothing in the world has authority over people's consciences except the Word of the Lord, and that Word has authority. It has the authority to bind consciences, to awe and terrify men.

So, a gracious heart sees the great seal of heaven stamped upon every truth in God's Word and therefore dares not trivialize it as it did before. It approaches the Word either as a sovereign to receive laws or as a judge to receive the sentence of condemnation. It regards the Word as backed with such authority that it must either yield to it or be bound over to eternal death, with bonds that no power of any creature in heaven or earth can release. When a soldier is rebuked by a fellow soldier, it doesn't bother him much. But if the general speaks, who holds his life in his hand, then he trembles. Similarly, when people come to hear the Word as coming from a minister whom they consider their equal, they don't pay much attention to it. But a gracious heart, regardless of the minister, regards the Word as superior. Cyprian calls it the tribunal of the church because that is where people receive the sentence of death upon themselves. When the soul sees this, it cannot help but tremble at whatever truths are revealed to it. That's the third aspect.

But fourthly, a gracious heart trembles at God's Word because it sees infinite justice in it, the justice of God that threatens eternal curse upon every soul that does not obey it in every aspect. In Deuteronomy 33:2, it is called a fiery law, a part of God's law, the fiery law of God. We know how the law was given with great dreadfulness, as can be seen in Exodus 19. The mountain shook and trembled when the law of God was given. And God expects the hearts of sinners to tremble when they hear the law of God at any time.

But you may ask, "We are delivered from it, so why should we tremble?"

However, even though we have been delivered, there is still a reason to tremble because we were once under the law, and we deserved to be under it. We read about Moses himself, a godly man who was in Christ, yet in Hebrews 12:21 it says that the sight was so terrible that Moses, the servant of God, said, "I exceedingly fear and quake." This is especially true if the soul does not fully understand that it has been completely delivered from the guilt of sin. The conscience will testify that the Word of God has an advantage over it. When Samuel came to Bethlehem, the elders of the town trembled at his coming, as mentioned in Ezra 16:2, it says, "The people sat trembling because of the matter." They had much guilt in them and knew that the Word had the advantage over them, so they trembled. It is important for everyone to tremble to some degree. That's the fourth aspect.

Fifthly, a gracious heart sees the Word of the Lord backed by infinite power. In Ecclesiastes 8:4, it says, "Where the word of a king is, there is power." Similarly, where the Word of the Lord is, there is power to fulfill it. In the latter end of Matthew 28, Jesus says, "All power in heaven and earth is given unto me." What follows? "Go therefore and preach." What can we observe from this connection? It implies that all the power in heaven and earth given to Jesus will accompany you while you are preaching His Word to fulfill the word that you preach. Therefore, whenever you hear any truth of God preached from His Word, know that all power in heaven and earth is sent forth to assist and fulfill it. Whether it is a threat to be fulfilled or a promise to be fulfilled, the power of God is at work.

In Isaiah 55:11, the Lord says that His Word shall not be in vain, it will not return empty, but in one way or another, it will accomplish the purpose for which He sent it. We may hope that God's intention in sending His Word to you has been out of mercy, but it will surely achieve some specific purpose that God has had among you. In Ezekiel 6:10, God declares, "They shall know that I am the Lord, and that I had not said in vain that I would do this evil to them." God wants every sinner to know that He is the Lord and that His words are not spoken in vain. It is as if God is saying, "If I am God, then My Word shall prevail and have an impact. All the power I possess will accompany My Word to fulfill it." We know from Matthew 5:18 that heaven and earth may pass away, but not one jot or tittle of God's Word will pass away. This reveals God's firm commitment to His Word. He would rather remove His power from upholding heaven and earth than withdraw His power from assisting His Word. If even one small truth (as you may consider it) has touched your conscience and made you ponder, "If this is true, what will become of me?" Pay attention, for heaven and earth may pass away, but God's Word will always be fulfilled. The Lord would rather lose the entire world than lose His Word.

Sixthly, a gracious heart sees the radiance of God's holiness, and being aware of its own impurity, it trembles. In Psalm 99:3, it says, "Let them praise your great and awesome name; Holy is He!" The name of God is great and awesome, and it is great and awesome because it is holy. The Word of God is nothing less than a reflection of His infinite holiness. When the brilliance of His holiness is revealed, it strikes fear into their hearts. In Isaiah 6, when the prophet heard the seraphim crying out, "Holy, holy, holy," the text says that even the blessed prophet himself cried out, "Woe is me, for I am undone!" The mere mention of the glory of God's holiness caused the prophet's heart to shake and tremble. Now, if a godly person trembles in this way, how much more should the hearts of those who are impure and corrupt tremble at the Word when they come to realize that it is a reflection of the holiness of the infinite God!

Seventhly, there is another aspect that must not be overlooked, and that is the glorious, lofty, and divine mysteries that are revealed in God's Word, which cause a gracious heart to tremble. In the Word of God, there are wondrous, exalted, and awe-inspiring mysteries that are disclosed—mysteries that should be approached with trembling. It is more fitting for humble creatures to receive them with reverence than to attempt to unravel them through inquiries. Oh, the mysteries of salvation! They are of such infinite magnitude that they cannot help but instill trembling in the hearts of those who come to comprehend their glory. There is the mystery of election, redemption, the hypostatic union, the death of the Son of God, justification, reconciliation, adoption, sanctification, and glorification. These are mysteries to be revered due to their unfathomable depth, length, height, and breadth.

Junius, the renowned theologian whose works have been a great blessing to the Church, recounts his own experience. He confesses that he was an atheist before his conversion. However, on a rainy day, as he returned home and noticed a New Testament lying before him, he picked it up and began to read. He came across the first chapter of John, which is filled with majestic words. He recalls, "As I read the book, my body trembled, and my soul was immediately astonished. I was so overwhelmed with horror and amazement that I shook in every part of my being, and my heart trembled within me. I was in a state of confusion and astonishment throughout the entire day, not knowing where I was."

And this was the means of the conversion of that renowned theologian: when God allowed a few rays of the gospel to shine upon his heart through His Word, his heart was struck with trembling, and it became the instrument of his soul's conversion. How many times have you read that chapter and heard other mysteries of the gospel without being so deeply affected! When the Lord intends to show favour to a soul, He reveals some of the profound mysteries found in His Word.

I have heard of a godly man, a great scholar, who was in his study, deeply engrossed in contemplating the glory of God as it manifested in the arts and sciences. For indeed, various arts are nothing more than glimpses of God's wisdom. While pondering this, he was so overwhelmed that he fell upon his face. Surely, these glorious mysteries ought to cause us to bow down, adore, and tremble before the Lord even more intensely.

In heaven, it will be the grand occupation of the saints and angels to stand in awe and marvel at these splendid mysteries of the gospel. The soul not only trembles at the demands of strictness found in God's Word but also at the awe-inspiring mysteries contained within it.

Eighthly, furthermore, a gracious heart trembles at the Word because it finds it to be exceedingly effective and powerful. The Word is likened to a two-edged sword, remarkably alive wherever it goes, as stated in Hebrews 4:12 and onwards. "For the word of God is quick and powerful, sharper than any two-edged sword, piercing even to the dividing asunder of soul and spirit, and of the joints and marrow, and is a discerner of the thoughts and intents of the heart," and so on. The Word of God operates with vivacity, working within the soul with great swiftness, leading towards either heaven or hell. This is why it is a Word to be trembled at. It is not the same for people when the Word comes with power as it was before. In the days of ignorance, God overlooked certain things. Thus, in the very first commission that Christ gives to His apostles, to go and preach, He declares, "Go you, and preach the Gospel to every creature; he that believeth shall be saved; he that believeth not, shall be damned." You can see how prompt Christ is. If they come in and believe, even the greatest sinner of all shall be saved. Approach the most wicked sinner, if they come in, they shall be saved; if not, they shall be damned. The Lord deals with great swiftness with those who live under the powerful ministry of the Word. Therefore, when John the Baptist comes to preach, he declares, "Now is the axe laid to the root of the tree." Why now? Why not before? Because now John the Baptist has arrived among the people, and now their natural condition is being revealed to them, and they feel the Word speaking directly to their consciences. If they do not submit now, then the axe is laid to the root of the trees. They must not expect to go on as they did before. Perhaps they were old drunkards, habitual swearers, and they managed to escape consequences for a long time. But now they must not think they can continue to escape for long. Therefore, as the Apostle says, "The word is either the savour of life unto life, or else the savour of death unto death" (2 Corinthians 2:16). This may seem challenging to understand, so let us explain it a little further. He does not say that death comes to one and life to another, but rather the savour of death and the savour of life.

The meaning is this: It is derived from things that are so full of spirit and efficacy that even the very scent is enough to bring about life or death. If one were to encounter a medicine whose scent alone could revive someone from death to life, we would say it is a very potent substance, full of vitality. Well, the Word is so full of vitality that if it is embraced, it brings life through its very essence, but if not, it becomes the scent of death leading to death. Ambrose, in his commentary on the text, uses this expression: "They receive the Word as the Plague if they do not obey it." Just like the plague, the mere scent of it is enough to bring death. Similarly, the Word of God, when not obeyed, becomes like a plague to wicked and ungodly individuals, and its very essence destroys them. This means that when I come to hear the Word, I come to hear something so powerful that each sermon I listen to, I must expect to be either closer to heaven or closer to hell. If you have attended a sermon and left carelessly, without taking it seriously or reflecting upon it, ask yourself: Did this sermon bring me closer to heaven than before? If not, then you are closer to hell.

Ninthly, furthermore, it trembles at the Word because it recognizes that the Word determines everyone's eternal destiny. If you wish to know how it will be for you in eternity, if you simply examine the Word and pay attention to it, you can know. For the Word contains what determines the eternal fate of every human being. Therefore, the Word deserves great reverence. When a prisoner is being sentenced to life, they look upon those in power with a trembling heart, even if they know they are innocent and hope for a favorable verdict from the jury. However, when they look at the jury, they realize that these are the individuals who will decide their fate, and they cannot help but tremble. Similarly, if you understand the immense consequence of an eternal destiny, you cannot help but tremble. When you open the Book of God, you recognize that this is the book that will determine your eternal fate, so it is a Word to be trembled at.

Tenthly, yes, not only does it determine our eternal destiny, but it is also a probing Word that examines and scrutinizes us in the present. It delves into the innermost recesses and secrets of the heart, dividing between the marrow and the bones, and revealing the very thoughts within. When a wounded person has a surgeon examine their wound, they look upon them with a trembling heart.

And many can attest to it from their own experience. How often have I come to the Word of God and found it penetrating my very heart, reaching the depths of my soul beyond all superficiality, laying bare everything before the Lord. And oh, the trembling that follows for a long time thereafter. In 1 Corinthians 14:25, it is said, "And thus the secrets of his heart are revealed. So, falling down on his face, he will worship God and report that God is truly among you." This is spoken of a poor ignorant man who enters a congregation, initially curious and in awe, but eventually realizes that the secrets of his heart are being exposed. In response, he falls down in reverence to God, worships Him, and acknowledges that God is present in that place. Similarly, many men and women, when they come to hear the Word, do so with worldly and empty hearts. However, when they discover that the Word scrutinizes them, enters into their being, wrestles with them, and confronts the inward and hidden disorders of their spirits, they are compelled to bow before the Word and proclaim, "Truly, God is in this Word." This experience causes sinners to humble themselves, and those with gracious hearts have encountered this effect through the Word.

Lastly, a gracious heart trembles at God's Word because it recognizes that it will be opened to judge them on the great Day. It examines and probes the soul in the present and will be one of the books opened to judge all humanity on the final day. In John 12:48, it is written, "He who rejects me and does not receive my words has that which judges him—the word that I have spoken will judge him in the last day." The words you hear now will be called to account once again—every sermon you have heard, every truth that God has impressed upon your conscience will be summoned and will judge you on the great Day. If you consider the Word as the arbiter of judgment on the final Day, it cannot help but make you tremble. Oh, if a gracious heart perceives the depth of meaning in the Word of God as has been revealed, surely there is ample reason for it to tremble at the Word of God. Let us not condemn those who tremble. Even if you do not tremble, do not be surprised, for God has granted them a vision that He has not yet granted you. But when the time of God's love arrives for your souls, you too shall see.

A few words of application: If this is true, then you should realise, firstly, how little you have understood the Word of God all this time! Oh, how little have I personally grasped of all that has been explained! Yet, there are some who see, regardless of what you do. Sometimes, even great scholars fail to see this, those with exceptional intellects. But perhaps, it is a poor servant who does see. "I thank you, Father, Lord of heaven and earth," says Christ, "that you have hidden these things from the wise and understanding and revealed them to little children." Now, if you find that God has worked these things in your hearts and your hearts tremble at His Word, then praise God for it. This can greatly help you in facing other fears that you may have. Oh, we fear what malicious people can do! But if you fear God's Word, you need not fear anything else. But you may say, "I have much sinfulness and wickedness in my heart, and I find that I am unable to do what God's Word requires." This can bring you comfort in all your weaknesses. Even though you may not fulfill everything the Word requires, God knows that you have a heart that obeys His Word in some things as well as in others. The Lord accepts your trembling, even when you lack the ability to perform. "Then those who feared the LORD spoke with one another. The LORD paid attention and heard them, and a book of remembrance was written before him," says God, "for those who feared the LORD and esteemed his name. 'They shall be mine,' says the LORD of hosts, 'in the day when I make up my treasured possession, and I will spare them as a man spares his son who serves him.'" If you fear God, now you have a promise that even with many weaknesses, God will spare you as one spares his only child who serves him.

Secondly, there are numerous sources of consolation.

Certainly, if you tremble at God's Word, you will be comforted, even if you may not find comfort at this moment. If the Word of God can make your heart tremble, it will bring you comfort. Wait for it. There is as much comfort in the Word of God for your soul as there was terror. Look at the chapter where my text is, verse 2: "I will look to him who is humble and contrite in spirit and trembles at my word." So, what will happen to them? Verse 5: "Hear the word of the LORD, you who tremble at his word." God repeats it because He loves it so. Are there any poor individuals whose conscience can testify, "Now the Lord knows that, despite my many weaknesses, He has instilled the awe and fear of His Word in my heart"? Your brethren, who hated you and cast you out for the sake of my name, will say, "Let the LORD be glorified." But He will appear to your joy, and they will be put to shame. Why does He speak of this comfort? Why does He say, "Your brethren, who hated you and cast you out for the sake of my name, will say, 'Let the LORD be glorified'"? Among these people, there were some who had tender consciences and dared not do the things others did. Therefore, their brethren hated them and cast them out. And it was not only notorious wicked individuals, but they said, "Let the LORD be glorified." They claimed to desire God's glory just as much as you. Yet, they cast out their brethren. But the Lord would comfort those who were cast out, those who trembled at His Word and refused to yield to the things others did.

Is it not the same today, my brethren? Some were willing to yield to anything to preserve their possessions and avoid trouble. But there were others who trembled at God's Word and would risk anything rather than go against the Word of God in any way. Now these individuals were thrown into prison, and the pretext was, "Let God be glorified." Now hear this: He will appear to your joy, and they will be put to shame. Oh, how this has been fulfilled.

Those proud individuals who were cruel in their oppression and cast out their brethren, yet the faithful ones gave up everything and entrusted their cause to God. But in a short time, how God has appeared to our joy and their shame. The fulfillment of this scripture alone should make us cherish the Word of God. If our forefathers, who trembled at God's Word and endured much persecution, were alive to witness this fulfillment, it would be enough to astonish them and acknowledge God's goodness. They would exclaim, "The Word of the Lord is good, and the Lord is faithful to all His promises."

And whatever may be imposed upon you in the future, if anything is imposed upon you that the Word of God does not uphold, be cautious. One who trembles at God's Word dares not do anything that is not supported by God's Word. It will not be enough for you to say on the great Day of Jesus Christ, "Such and such great men did this and that, and they commanded me or persuaded me, so I followed their commands or examples." But someone who trembles at the Word of the Lord will not do so. Surely the Lord has individuals in this congregation who tremble at His Word. I can clearly see the serious intention you have towards the Word of the Lord that is being delivered. God looks upon those families and individuals in a parish who set such good examples, making it evident to others that their hearts are captivated by the authority of God's Word.

Whenever you come to hear, do not regard it as the word of men, but as the Word of God. Even if it seems harsh to you, know that it comes for your own good. And there is a reason you should do so. It is the Word from which you received your life, the immortal seed of the Word by which you were born again. I ask you, have you been born again or not? If you have been born again, it is the Word that has begotten you, and it is that Word which is the object of your faith for your souls and eternal state. Surely, it deserves your reverence.

Once again, the Word of God should be the foundation of all your prayers. Whenever you pray to God, if you do not base your prayers on the Word, it will be of little use. As David said, "Have mercy on me according to your Word." Furthermore, in times of affliction, the Word should be your source of comfort. Therefore, it is crucial that you reverence it now.

Indeed, if your souls are to be saved, it will be through the Word. Therefore, be cautious not to despise it. Oh, it will weigh heavily on your conscience, both on your sickbed and deathbed! Fear the Word of God now!

You may say, "We will fear the Word of God," but is everything a person says considered the Word of God? We know that individuals hold different opinions.

To that, I respond, when something is presented in God's name, do not dismiss it lightly. Instead, test and examine it. Suppose someone comes to you with the official seal; will you say, "I don't recognize it as the official seal, so I won't obey it"? Doing so may cost you your possessions or even something dear to you. Similarly, when something is presented in the name of God, do not dismiss it without consideration. Rather, examine it and test it against the Scriptures to determine if it aligns with the divine standard.

I knew a gentleman who, upon returning home from a sermon, said, "Well, if what this minister says is true, then we are in a bad situation." Woe to the person whose primary comfort relies on the false belief that what they hear from the Word is not actually the Word. That individual is in a wretched state, having no other foundation for their comfort. However, you may ask, "Should we accept everything that is taught?"

No, not without discernment. In the book of Acts, they were commended for examining whether what Paul delivered to them was true. It is indeed commendable for people to scrutinise whether what a minister imparts is truly the Word of God.

Yet, some of us are poor and ignorant individuals, you might say.

Therefore, I want to address the most ignorant among you and guide you on how to distinguish the Word of God from other teachings.

Firstly, if you desire to know, approach with a heart willing to submit to what you come to understand. As stated in John 7:17, "If anyone chooses to do God's will, they will find out whether my teaching comes from God or whether I speak on my own." If you have a heart surrendered to God, willing to obey, you will discern whether the doctrine being presented is from God or merely human. There is a promise—make use of it.

Secondly, plead this promise before the Lord. Find a solitary place, cry out to God, and implore Him to reveal the truth to you. Go and pray, saying, "Lord, I have heard certain things spoken, and it seems they are touching my heart, but I am feeble and ignorant. If it is Your Word, Lord, make it resonate in my heart."

Another rule to follow is this: if you are able to read, search the Scriptures. Seek out your neighbours and approach the ministers, striving to understand the reasons behind the teachings given to you. This applies even to the most ignorant individuals. They have no excuse unless they come with hearts surrendered to God and make use of every possible means to comprehend the Word of God. And when you attend sermons to hear the Word, endeavour to maintain a constant state of trembling in your hearts. The Word that you currently tremble at will, from that moment onwards, bring comfort to your heart.

# Chapter Two

# SERMON II

## What the True Sanctified Fear of God and His Word is.

—And that trembleth at my Word. -Isaiah. 66.2.

I will not repeat anything, but rather reflect on other aspects of this significant and weighty matter that concerns us so closely.

The heart that trembles at God's Word is regarded with fondness by God; it is very pleasing in His sight.

But you may argue, "Even the devils believe and tremble" (James 2:19). In this regard, they surpass many miserable and audacious sinners, whom we will discuss in the application later. We also read about Felix, who was an infamous wicked man, trembling at the Word (Acts 24:25). As Paul reasoned about righteousness, temperance, and judgment to come, Felix trembled. Felix, a judge sitting on the bench, and Paul, a lowly prisoner at the bar. Yet, through his preaching on righteousness, temperance, and judgment to come, Paul made the judge tremble on his seat. This demonstrates the power of the Word. It is worth noting that in the preceding verse, it is mentioned that Felix came with his wife

Drusilla, who was a Jewess. It is curious why his wife is specifically mentioned here.

Interpreters refer to the Jewish story of that time, which tells us that Drusilla, Felix's wife, was previously married to another man. Because Felix was a man of great honour, she left her previous husband and even her religion to marry him. So now, the text says, "As he reasoned of righteousness," targeting Felix, a corrupt judge, "and temperance," addressing his immorality as a womanizer, "Drusilla, who was present, was a vile, wicked, unclean woman." Therefore, he spoke of temperance and discussed things that would strike closest to their consciences. And he also spoke of judgment to come, reminding the judge and his Delilah that both of them would one day stand before the Almighty God to give an account. Felix would answer for his injustice, and both he and Drusilla would answer for the filthiness in which they lived. This illustrates the Apostle's boldness. Although he was a prisoner, he spoke words that would deeply affect those he addressed, knowing full well that he would provoke them both.

It is said that Felix trembled, but we do not read the same of his wife. In fact, if women give themselves to impurity, they become even more hardened. Felix, though a wicked and ungodly man, was compelled to tremble at Paul's preaching. Now, you may argue, "If even the devils tremble, and Felix can tremble, how does it prove that a heart that trembles at God's Word is so pleasing to God?" A poor trembling heart may say, "I'm afraid that my trembling and fear are only in response to the threat of God's Word. I hear about the coming judgment, and I tremble, but what does that amount to? It's nothing."

Answer: Regarding that, I respond: Nothing, yet that's something. Firstly, it is a sign that the Word has exerted more power over your hearts than before.

Secondly, it is something. It involves placing fear upon the right object, and that's significant. Even if there isn't a gracious principle to fully act upon that object as it should, setting fear upon the right object is still meaningful.

Yes, thirdly, trembling in this manner is somewhat significant. It can prevent a great deal of evil and keep you free from many temptations. Even the trembling of your heart can strengthen you against temptations.

Fourthly, it is even more significant because it may serve as preparation for additional good that God intends for you.

Objection: But you might argue that this could be the extent of it, and nothing more.

Answer: Yes, but first, understand that no one who has grace can be without this to some extent. Although some who have this trembling may lack grace, no one who possesses grace can be without it.

Objection: You might say, "Yes, it is possible for some to be brought to Christ without experiencing trembling."

Answer: To that, I respond, when a soul is brought to Christ, why does it embrace Him? Why does it believe in Him and rely upon Him? Is it not to reconcile the dreadful separation between God and the soul through Christ the Mediator? And can the soul be aware of this and not tremble? Certainly, it cannot help but tremble. Therefore, although it may be absent where there is no grace, where there is grace, this trembling exists.

Secondly, understand that this disposition of the heart (and even to this extent you have reached) is what God uses to work in those whom He intends to bring good to in the end.

Objection: But you may argue that some may have this trembling and yet not be saved. They may perish in the end, even though they have a degree of fear when faced with the threats in God's Word.

Answer: To that, I reply, it is true that there may be trembling in response to the threats in the Word of God, and yet the soul may fail to find salvation. Not only may it lack saving grace in the present, but it may never attain it at all. However, know that there is a significant difference between the trembling that God brings to a positive outcome and the trembling that ultimately leads to nothing.

I will demonstrate this distinction and then proceed to explain what true, sanctified trembling at God's Word entails.

But first, let's consider even the trembling at God's threats. There is a significant difference when you put together these four or five aspects that I am currently discussing. You will see a clear distinction between the fear that leads to nothing and the fear that God ultimately brings to something. Those who possess these five characteristics, when combined, exhibit a trembling that, I believe, has never failed to yield positive outcomes.

Firstly, when the trembling (although initially triggered by the threats in God's Word, it surpasses all other fears), I mean in terms of its intensity. Two factors contribute to the intensity of fear in the heart:

First, the magnitude of the evil.

Secondly, the difficulty of overcoming that evil.

If the evil is trivial, the heart disregards it. Even if the evil is great, if it can be easily avoided, the human heart tends to dismiss it. However, when these two factors are combined—an immense evil that is exceedingly challenging to avoid—the heart experiences fear. Now, the soul that is brought to trembling comprehends the breach between God and itself, recognizing the profound evil of sin as revealed in the Word, the greatest evil of all. It develops a new perception of the difficulty involved in reconciling with God. The Word reveals that establishing peace with God is an infinitely arduous task, and based on this understanding, the soul trembles with a fear that surpasses all other fears and trembling.

Secondly, (because we must not consider any of these signs in isolation) it is consumed by great fear to the extent that it justifies God. And here lies a significant distinction indeed, for if you only consider the magnitude of fear on its own, it may exist in some who may perish. But when you add to it the other aspect—that in this profound fear, when the soul trembles at what the Lord has revealed in His Word—the soul justifies God and His Word entirely. Despite the Word speaking dreadful things against me, the Word of God is just, and God is righteous in His Word. The soul humbles itself and justifies God in all the severity that He unveils in His Word against the sins of which the soul is conscious. When the heart reaches this point, it truly enters a hopeful condition. There are many who are compelled to tremble, but they resent God and complain about the justice of God and His Word. However, when the Lord strikes the heart with fear and causes the soul to justify Him and His Word, then the soul is truly on the right path.

Thirdly, this heart not only fears the threats of God's wrath but also fears the evil of departing from God and losing His presence—the loss of communion with God, being forever cast out from the Lord, never to behold His face or experience His goodness. This is revealed in the Word, and the soul trembles at it just as it does at the concept of Hell. Many carnal hearts may tremble upon hearing about the threats of Hell and eternal fire, but for the heart to tremble at the thought of God departing from it and being rejected by the Holy and Blessed God—oh, that is a very positive sign when the heart trembles at this.

Fourthly, the heart trembles at the Word of God to such an extent that nothing can calm it, nothing can satisfy it except Reconciliation with God. When the heart is struck with this fear and trembling, nothing can satisfy it except being reconciled with God Himself. Whatever God may propose to it, it can never find contentment. Some may tremble at God's Word in times of sickness, but if they regain their health, they are at peace. They tremble in afflictions, but in prosperity, they are calm. However, the heart that is struck with the fear that God intends to bring it to good will never find peace in anything other than reconciliation with God.

Fifthly, this fear is not one that drives the heart away from God or causes it to resort to worldly solutions, nor does it lead to despair and fleeing from God. Instead, it is a fear that brings the heart to God, compelling it powerfully towards Him. The fear and trembling that result in despair or prevent one from entering God's presence are experienced by some reprobates, but the fear that drives the heart to God— the greater the fear, the more forcefully it propels the heart towards God—this is a good sign that this fear and trembling is genuine. So, when you consider these five aspects together—the fact that your fear is the greatest fear that overshadows all other fears, that you justify God in this fear, that you fear departing from God as well as His wrath, that nothing can calm you except reconciliation, and that this fear does not push you away from God but draws you towards Him—I must say, where can an example be found of any soul that has failed in this situation? I won't claim that this very thing is saving grace, but I will say that in the Scriptures, whenever this work has been present, the Lord has taken the soul further. However, we have yet to explain what the trembling is that is presently acceptable in the sight of God, what the true sanctified trembling at the Word of God is, which only a gracious heart possesses.

To that, I shall answer with these points. It is indeed essential for our spiritual growth to understand the true sanctified work of fear in the heart, when the soul fears God and His Word.

What the true sanctified fear of God and His Word is:

First, it is an active fear in the soul. Please pay attention to this. By that, I mean that it is not a fear that is forced or imposed upon the heart. The Lord goes beyond that. The soul has an inner principle that drives this fear. What I mean is this: the Lord has enabled my heart to perceive something in His Word that makes me tremble, and I am grateful for it. I am glad that I am aware of the Word, that it has been revealed to me, and that it has evoked such a response in me. The heart now acts upon this fear and regards it as a mercy that the Word, which causes fear and trembling, has been revealed. It does not view it as an evil or a misery, as many people do when they hear the Word that makes their hearts tremble. They see it as a plague, and they may even express resentment towards the Word and the ministers who proclaim it, just as those possessed once cried out to Christ, "Have you come to torment us before the appointed time?"

They make every effort to push away the thoughts that may evoke this fear in their hearts. They believe that if they can rid their conscience of the Word that the Lord has impressed upon them through His ministry, then they will be safe. However, they become vexed and agitated because they cannot sleep peacefully since hearing such a message. They cannot eat, drink, or go about their daily tasks calmly. They consider it a form of bondage and misery that their hearts are so sensitive to the Word of God. However, it is different for a gracious heart. The Lord causes fear and trembling in a gracious heart, and this heart blesses God for making it sensitive to His Word. It regards it as a favour from God and strives to maintain this fear and trembling within. It gathers whatever arguments it can to cultivate this fear in the heart. "Unite my heart to the fear of Your name" - you know it is the prayer of David and the Church. "Lord, you have begun to make me aware of the authority and majesty of Your Word. I am afraid that I will lose this fear. Lord, unite my heart to the fear of Your name. Lord, instil this fear in my heart." Just as it was said of Daniel (a passage I previously referred to on a different occasion), "My thoughts greatly troubled me, and my countenance changed, but I kept the matter in my heart." Yes, this was a sign of a gracious heart in that situation. Although the circumstances may differ from what we are currently discussing, it can still be applicable to us. How few people in this congregation (or any congregation, for that matter) act in this way? You may come to hear what is preached, and you cannot deny the truth of those things. They may be spoken in a convincing manner, causing your thoughts to trouble you and your countenance to change. Do you keep these matters in your heart? No, rather, your endeavour is to push them out of your heart. I recall hearing once about a very carnal and wretched man who, by chance, heard a sermon that strongly affected him. He confessed, "I couldn't get the word out of my conscience for an entire week after that man spoke." However, a gracious heart retains it in their conscience. This is true trembling when the heart is active. It is not a forced work, but the soul embraces these truths.

Secondly, as the soul is active in it, it is also made active by it. There is much significance in this. When fear strikes a hypocrite upon hearing the Word, they are often overcome by that fear. If they do not despair, they are still discouraged and disheartened, lacking the motivation to do anything. However, the fear of the godly is different. It enlarges their souls towards God and activates their hearts for Him. It enables them to be ready for their duties and does not render them unfit, as the fear of the hypocrite does. We have a remarkable passage in Ezra 9:3 as evidence. "And when I heard this, I tore my garment and my robe, pulled hair from my head and beard, and sat down appalled." Observe how deeply troubled the righteous man was when he witnessed the disobedience to the Word of the Lord. He was astonished and greatly distressed. Then in verse 5, "And at the evening sacrifice I rose from my fasting, with my garment and my robe torn, and fell upon my knees and spread out my hands to the Lord my God." He proceeded to offer a gracious prayer. From this, we learn a valuable lesson: Souls that are struck with the fear of God and His Word in a godly manner are not hindered in their duties; instead, they are enlarged. It enlarges their hearts and makes them more active for God, even more so than before. Fear and enlargement can coexist. In Jeremiah 33:9, "And they shall fear and tremble because of all the good and all the prosperity I provide for it." In Isaiah 60:5, we find both expressions together, fear and enlargement. When the heart is struck with the fear of God, yet simultaneously experiences enlargement, becoming active and suitable for service, this is a sign of a gracious trembling that God accepts. God pays less attention to the horror that paralyzes and renders people unfit for service. Instead, He values the enlargement and readiness that make them fit for service.

Thirdly, this gracious trembling at God's Word is joined with love. It is a combination of fear and love. It trembles at the Word, yet it loves the Word. It remains committed to hearing the Word, even though it trembles. It stands by the Word, even if others speak against it. Typically, people who are feared are not loved; they are hated by those who fear them. However, a sincere disposition desires to be both loved and feared. An hypocrite may be brought to fear and tremble at God's Word, but they never love it. Fear and love do not coexist within them. They fear God's Word, but they hate it. They wish there were no such Word of God, and that it was not as strict and holy as it is. In other words, they wish God were not so holy, which is essentially wishing there were no God at all. Yet, a wicked heart is so infatuated with its lusts that it would rather have no God at all than be without its lusts. This is exemplified in the case of Ahab. He trembled, yet he hated the Word of God and the prophet. The story of Ahab in 1 Kings 22:8 is well-known. When Ahab was going to Ramoth Gilead, he said to Jehoshaphat, "There is yet one man, Michaiah the son of Imlah, by whom we may inquire of the Lord, but I hate him, for he never prophesies good concerning me, but evil." Jehoshaphat responded, "Let not the king say so." I mention this incident to compare it with Ahab's disposition in Chapter 21. Ahab admitted that there was one prophet of the Lord, but he said, "I hate him." However, towards the end of the chapter, when the prophet came to him to speak the Word of the Lord, Ahab was struck with fear and trembling. The text states that when Ahab heard those words, he tore his clothes, put sackcloth on his flesh, fasted, and went about mourning. This is the same Ahab who trembled at the Word of God and humbled himself, yet in the next chapter, he says, "There is one prophet of the Lord, but I hate him." Ahab trembled before the prophets of God, yet he hated them. In contrast, a gracious heart trembles at the Word of God and loves it. It rejoices in it as a good Word, especially directed to the individual. This serves as a third proof.

Fourthly, true fear and trembling at the Word is that which will settle the heart and strengthen it against all other fears. It will overshadow greater fears. But its virtue lies in its ability to fortify the heart and enable it to withstand all other fears. For example, a heart that trembles at the Word, though afraid at that moment, is not greatly afraid of outward losses and afflictions in the world. A notable example can be found in Habakkuk 3. There we see a prophet whose heart trembled greatly at God's Word when he heard it. In verse 16, he says, "When I heard, my belly trembled; my lips quivered at the voice; rottenness entered into my bones, and I trembled in myself." You might think, "Surely Habakkuk was a very fearful man." However, you will discover that he was not a fearful man. He had a strong and courageous spirit, and this trembling at God's Word actually strengthened his spirit and made him courageous in the face of outward afflictions. In verse 17, he declares, "Although the fig tree shall not blossom, neither shall fruit be in the vines; the labour of the olive shall fail, and the fields shall yield no food; the flock shall be cut off from the fold, and there shall be no herd in the stalls." This refers to a dreadful famine and a dire situation. Yet, his heart, which had experienced such fear before, now fears none of these things. Many of you do not tremble at God's Word, but you tremble at the fear of any loss. You tremble at people, but not at the Word of God. However, true and gracious trembling at God's Word strengthens the heart against other fears. David also experienced this in Psalm 119:161. He says, "Princes have persecuted me without cause, but my heart stands in awe of your word." It is as if he is saying, "This is what will help me. Princes set themselves against me and persecute me unjustly, but my heart will stand in awe of your Word. The fear of your Word in my heart will prevent me from fearing the persecutions of the mighty in the world. I stand in awe of your Word." In other words, there are a group of cowardly individuals who may appear courageous in other matters, but when it comes to persecution, they will yield to anything. What causes them to do so? It is because their hearts were never struck with the fear of God's Word. But I do not fear greatly. Why? Because I have another fear in my heart that strengthens me against that fear. Therefore, this trembling at God's Word is what helps the soul overcome all other tremblings.

And by the way, do not think it is a difficult lesson to teach you to tremble at God's Word. What, does it bring fear to us? It brought peace at first. No, it is the way to cure you of all base fears. If you never fear humans, losses, afflictions, or troubles, then fear the Word of God and tremble at that. The more fear there is of God's Word, the less fear there will be of any creature in the world. It is the only way to free you from all fears whatsoever.

Fifthly, another characteristic is this: true and gracious trembling at God's Word is accompanied by joy. It is joined with love, as mentioned before, but joy is a higher degree. In the sanctification of the heart, there is a blessed mixture of love and joy. Just like in exquisite works where gold, silver, and pearls are combined, making it beautiful, the grace of sanctification is a masterpiece. So it is with fear and joy. You are familiar with the verse in Psalm 2:11, "Rejoice with trembling." The soul trembles at the Word, yet it is glad that such a Word of God exists. The soul considers the Word of God to be its inheritance. We have an excellent scripture to support this in Deuteronomy 33:2, which says, "From his right hand went a fiery law." But pay attention to what follows in verse 40, "Moses commanded us a law, even the inheritance of the congregation of Jacob." What? A fiery law and yet an inheritance?

Yes, even if it has great severity. Take note of verse 3: He commanded a fiery law, yet He loved the people. You must not think that when a minister preaches things that seem dreadful to you, it means he does not love you. Pay attention here, God gave a fiery law, and yet He loved them. People should sit with meekness, quietness, and humility at your feet, receiving your words, even if it is a fiery law. And then in verse 4, Moses commanded us a law, even the inheritance of the congregation of Jacob. Oh, even though the law is fiery, we consider it to be our inheritance in the law. Therefore, those who want to completely take away the law from us would be taking away part of our inheritance. Therefore, trembling and joy can coexist. In Psalm 119:162, we have a similar but more explicit verse: "I rejoice at thy word, as one that findeth great spoil." If you were traveling and came across a great booty, you would rejoice. Well, a gracious heart can rejoice at God's word as much as anyone in the world who finds great spoils. Therefore, when we urge you to fear God's word, we are not enemies of your joy. The truth is, the only way to have true joy is to tremble at the word of God.

Sixthly, a gracious trembling is a habitual trembling: a trembling of the heart that is present in the heart as a habit, not only in sudden moments. Many times God strikes some sudden flashes of terror into the hearts of men and women, but they vanish and amount to nothing. But this trembling at God's word, which the Lord highly values, is a constant and habitual disposition of the soul. It is not limited to certain instances of perceiving God's displeasure. Let God speak peace to the soul (please take note of this point), even if God speaks peace abundantly to this soul, it continues to tremble at the word of God. God's assurance of peace does not remove this disposition of the heart. Even when the conscience is most at peace, it still trembles at the word of God. Many people tremble at God's word during times of sickness and affliction, but as soon as they have tranquility and outward peace, their trembling disappears. However, a gracious heart trembles at the word of God even when the conscience is most at peace. It is an excellent indication of truth and genuine peace if you can experience this trembling when your conscience is most calm. We find an excellent scripture in Daniel 10:11: "And he said unto me, O Daniel, a man greatly beloved, understand the words that I speak unto thee, and stand upright." Here was a message of abundant mercy to Daniel, and the Lord, through an angel, affirmed that Daniel was greatly beloved. The Lord sent the angel to instruct him according to His will. Pay attention, "For unto thee am I now sent." And when he spoke these words to me, I stood trembling. Despite receiving this testimony from God at that very moment, that he was a man greatly beloved, and the angel was sent to inform him that his prayer was heard, Daniel still stands trembling. He stands with reverence and fear before the Lord, ready to listen to His word. This is how it will be with a gracious heart. Even when there is the greatest testimony of acceptance from God, and when there is peace in the spirit, it still approaches the word and stands trembling before it.

Seventhly, and lastly, it is a fear that subdues the heart to the power of the word. It subdues the thoughts, opinions, conscience, will, and affections to the power of the word. It is the kind of fear that struck Saul's heart at his conversion in Acts 9:6. Here we see true trembling. He trembled and was astonished, saying, "Lord, what do you want me to do?" Regardless of my previous opinions, regardless of my past ways, and regardless of the stubbornness and obstinacy in my heart, Lord, no more, no more. You have struck my heart with fear. When God, through His word, strikes down the heart of a man or woman and causes them to tremble as Saul did here, crying out, "Lord, what do you want me to do?" This is a gracious trembling, and the Lord pays special attention to it. Oh, the one who trembles at the word of God in this way is dear and precious in God's sight.

Now, you may wonder, why does the Lord have such a special regard for a trembling heart?

Why, first of all, it is because this disposition glorifies God's Word. When people come and listen to it with frivolous and vain spirits, and perhaps make jokes about it afterwards, and speak of it lightly, they dishonour the Word of God. But when the Lord sees a group of humble creatures coming to hear His Word and trembling before it, apprehending the truths I have explained to you, then the Lord sees His Word being honoured. God Himself loves to bestow great honour upon His Word, and therefore He loves those who honour His Word as well. In Isaiah 42, we read that He loves to make His law honourable. In verse 21, it says, "The LORD is well pleased for his righteousness' sake; he will magnify the law and make it honourable." Even if people may despise it, God will make His law honourable. The Lord loves to see His creatures magnifying and honouring His Word.

And are you someone who trembles at God's Word? You are, in a sense, assisting God in the great thing He delights to do. When a group of people glorifies God's Word, as we see in another instance in the Book of Acts where it says, "They glorified the word of God," oh, the Lord loves that. This disposition of the heart glorifies the Word of God, which is dearer to Him than anything except His Son. As Christ said, "Heaven and earth will pass away, but not one jot or tittle of my word will pass away." Now, you, who honour God's Word, oh, you are accepted in God's sight.

Secondly, this disposition of heart puts a great deal of honour upon God. His name is greatly sanctified when the heart trembles at His Word. It shows honour to His wisdom, sovereignty, majesty, authority, and holiness.

The truth is, the Lord is more honoured by a heart trembling at His Word than by a heart trembling at any glorious manifestations of Himself in all His works. For instance, let's suppose the Lord comes and appears from heaven in glory, accompanied by thunder, lightning, and earthquakes. Imagine Him appearing as He will on the great Day of Judgment, with the heavens departing like a scroll and the firmament melting with fervent heat. At that moment, perhaps all of you would tremble in fear at the great Day of Judgment. However, my brethren, for a soul to tremble at God's Word glorifies God even more than trembling at His glorious manifestation on that day. Why? Because the latter is such a display of God's power that it would naturally elicit fear from us. But this trembling at His Word comes from a gracious and sanctified frame within the heart of a person. God considers Himself more glorified by this trembling than He will be on that day. Therefore, those of you who do not want to tremble with horror and despair on that day, tremble now at God's Word. If you do so, you need not fear that all those glorious manifestations of God will overwhelm your hearts with horror on the great Day of Judgment.

Why? Because God has already received the glory of His name through your fear of Him, even more than He would have received through any horror He could strike into you on the Day of Judgment. God says, "Why should I forcefully extract my glory from these poor creatures by instilling horror in them through a magnificent manifestation? For I have merely revealed myself to them in my Word, and their hearts have trembled and given glory to me." In Psalm 29, the Psalmist describes the voice of the Lord as thunder, portraying it as the most dreadful sound. God receives much glory through thundering and lightning, and by causing mighty oaks to quake and tremble. In Joel 3:16, it is written,

"The voice of the Lord shakes the heavens and the earth." When God chooses to reveal His glory, He does so through His powerful voice. However, God receives even more glory by shaking an immortal soul through His Word than by shaking the heavens and the earth. It is true that if God were to speak a single word, He could shake this building, heaven, and earth. But He would not receive as much glory by shaking them as He does through one immortal soul that trembles in the manner that has been explained to you. Oh, it is no wonder that God pays attention to such an individual, for His Word and even Himself are honoured and glorified by them.

# Chapter Three

# SERMON III

## A Broken, an Humble Heart

*And he that trembleth at my Word. Isai. 66.2.*

The Lord pays special attention to a trembling heart. Why? Because just as His Word is honoured and His name is sanctified, the Lord sees that the heart is broken, serious, and teachable, and therefore it must be accepted by God. It is a broken and humble heart, and that's why it is added that it is a contrite and broken heart that trembles at God's Word. These qualities are intertwined. The Lord takes great delight in a broken heart, which is the root of trembling at the Word of God. The reason why people do not fear and tremble at the Word of God is due to the pride and hardness of their hearts. However, an humble and broken heart is precious before God, and it is the source of this trembling.

Furthermore, it is a serious heart, and God loves a serious disposition. When a person has dealings with God, especially in serious matters, they need to be serious themselves. God cannot tolerate a frivolous and vain heart; it is a dreadful curse upon people's spirits. But when the heart starts to be serious, focusing on God and His truths in a serious manner, there is great hope for such an individual.

And it is highly teachable. A heart that trembles at the Word of God is teachable. In Acts 13:16, Paul says, "You who fear God, listen." It is as if he is saying, "I know you will pay attention to what is said." Only those who have the fear of God are truly fit to hear the Word, as it is the beginning of wisdom, according to Scripture. When men and women have the fear of God in their hearts, they begin to have wise hearts and understand God's Word. When their hearts tremble before the Word of God, they come to understand it. On the other hand, if their hearts are bold and presumptuous, they come and go from the Word without understanding anything. But when the heart trembles, it becomes teachable. That is why, before the Lord instructed Job, He first struck him with fear.

In Proverbs 15:33, the text says, "The fear of the Lord is the instruction of wisdom." Note that it is not only the beginning of wisdom but also the instruction of wisdom. This means that wisdom will never instruct a soul that does not have the fear of the Lord. It begins with the fear. Unless the Lord causes the heart to fear before Him, it will not be instructed, not even by wisdom itself. The jailer, who was rough and unyielding before, in Acts 16:29, came trembling and fell down before Paul and Silas, asking, "Sirs, what must I do to be saved?" Now the jailer is in a teachable disposition as he trembles and seeks guidance on salvation. When people ask questions in a trembling manner, they are in a teachable disposition. This is a precious state of spirit because it signifies a serious and teachable heart.

We now proceed to the application.

Firstly, we learn from this that God's judgment is not the same as human judgment. What is precious to God may not be considered precious by humans, and vice versa. Men tend to value bold and courageous spirits, those who are confident and full of vigour. They admire those who are fearless and dismissive of whatever the Word may say. On the other hand, those who tremble with fear and are troubled in conscience, those who are humble, broken, and troubled in spirit, are looked down upon and despised by the world. But God sees it differently. God considers the trembling heart to be the blessed and happy one. The world may despise those who shake and tremble at the Word because it does not align with the boldness valued by society. However, for a poor soul who trembles before God at His Word, God says, "To this person will I look." There is nothing in Heaven or Earth that pleases God more than someone who trembles before Him. But let us not dwell on this further.

Secondly, if this disposition is highly regarded by God, it should teach the ministers of God who have to deal with His Word to speak it in a manner that evokes fear and trembling, causing the hearts of people to be struck with fear and trembling. They must not approach it lightly or play with people's imaginations or their own cleverness. When they speak the Word of God in His name, they should strive to deliver it in such a way that the hearts of their listeners are filled with fear and trembling. There is indeed a way of speaking the Word of God that brings it with majesty to the hearts of the people. The Apostle Paul states in 1 Corinthians 2:4 concerning the ministry of the Word, "My speech and my preaching were not with enticing words of man's wisdom, but in demonstration of the Spirit and of power." Here we see two types of preaching: preaching with enticing words of human wisdom, which may earn a preacher praise for being clever, witty, or sophisticated, and preaching in the demonstration of the Spirit and of power. The power of the Word follows the demonstration of the Spirit. When people perceive a minister only preaching wit and showcasing their abilities, the heart may despise it. It may commend the person but despise the Word because it lacks power over the conscience. However, when a minister of God comes in His name and preaches in the demonstration of the Spirit, they preach with power that prevails with people's consciences. This is the demonstration of the Spirit and of power. It is said of Christ in Matthew 7:29 that He did not preach like the scribes and Pharisees but as one who had authority. The scribes and Pharisees had a superficial way of preaching, but Christ spoke with authority that reached people's consciences. Similarly, ministers of Christ should speak in His name, backed by His authority, as those who have to deal with people's consciences and not their fancies. Indeed, the best commendation of a sermon is when it strikes the hearts of people. When writing about Basil and Chrysostom, two famous preachers of their time, it is said that their true honour was not in the applause of the crowd but in people coming to them and crying out, "What must I do to be saved?" This is the commendation of a minister. Ministers should strive for their ministry to be of such a nature because the Lord highly values a heart that trembles at His Word.

There is enough substance in the Word of God to cause any heart to tremble, if it is delivered as the Word of God. What significance does worthless chaff hold compared to valuable wheat? In 1 Peter 4:11, it is stated, "If anyone speaks, they should do so as one who speaks the very words of God." If anyone takes it upon themselves to speak God's Word, it must be done as if speaking the Word of God, the divine oracles.

I recall reading about Cicero (Tully), who spoke with such power that he made Caesar's book fall out of his hand. And surely, if Cicero could have such an effect with his eloquence, there is even greater power and eloquence in the Word of God that can cause the desires and lusts of people to fall out of their hearts. The weapons we use in our spiritual battle are powerful through God's strength, capable of tearing down strongholds and proud imaginations that defy God and His truth. The Word of God possesses a divine power that is not of the flesh but of the Spirit, enabling it to cast down arrogant thoughts and make them tremble before the Lord. This concludes the second application.

Thirdly, from this gracious disposition of the heart, trembling at the Word, you can understand the reason why the servants of God are so obedient to His Word and dare not act against it. God has instilled in them a trembling at His Word, a perception that others do not possess. You may wonder why some individuals are so strict in their adherence to God's Word, why they would endure anything in the world rather than go against even a single sentence in the Word. You find it perplexing. The reason is that you do not perceive the majesty and authority in God's Word as they do. Your hearts have not been struck with fear and trembling. However, they perceive such majesty and fear in the Word that they dare not go against it. They would rather endure any hardship in the world than act contrary to the Word. They dare not do what you dare to do. In Revelation 6:9, it is said of some, "When he opened the fifth seal, I saw under the altar the souls of those who had been slain because of the word of God and the testimony they had maintained." In other words, they would rather be killed than go against the Word of God. They would remain faithful to the Word regardless of what happened to their lives and possessions. I saw those souls, and they were under the altar, under God's protection. Surely, they were individuals who trembled at the Word of God, and God looks upon such souls. The soul of such an individual shall lie under the altar, within God's sight, because they tremble and would rather lose their lives and everything than act against God's Word. This concludes the third point.

Fourthly, the fourth point is one of comfort and encouragement for all those who possess such a blessed disposition, those who tremble at the Word. "To him will I look, even to him who is poor and of a contrite spirit, and trembles at my word." The very text is filled with richness and offers comfort to such individuals. In the realm of nature, they say that "Tremor Cordis" is a disease, the trembling of the heart. However, in the realm of divinity, it is not a disease but a truly gracious disposition. Those who possess such a blessed disposition can find great comfort in it. Comfort can flow into their souls through various channels. There are six or seven streams of consolation flowing into the hearts of those who tremble at God's Word.

The first point is this: Surely, God has begun to enlighten your soul by allowing you to see His glory in His Word. This is a great mercy. There was a time when you saw nothing special in the Word of God, considering it no different from the words of man or other things. But has God now started to reveal His majesty and glory in His Word to you? Oh, this is a precious mercy! It signifies that God is beginning to work great things in your soul.

Secondly, if you have a heart that trembles at the Word, know that all the threats in God's Word have already had their impact on your soul. Therefore, you need not fear any harm from them. I repeat, you do not need to fear the execution of any threats found in God's Word. Why? Because God has already achieved the glory He desires from those threats within your heart. Why does the Lord threaten sinners in His Word? It is so that He may receive glory and that sinners may fear Him. But now, if you do fear Him and give Him glory, God has accomplished His purpose in issuing those threats, and they no longer have any power over you. It is a great comfort for a soul to know that no threatening in God's Word is directed at them to bring any harm upon them. Why? Because those threats have already achieved their purpose in my life, though not in execution.

There are two purposes for threats: either God obtains glory through their execution, or He receives glory through the trembling of the heart before Him.

Now, if God can receive His glory through your trembling, He will never desire to obtain His glory through execution. When He takes glory through execution, it is not because He delights in crushing the prisoners of the Earth under His feet. Indeed, God takes pleasure in His own glory. He is determined to receive glory for His name from every creature. However, God prefers to obtain His glory from our souls in an active manner rather than forcefully extracting glory from us in a passive manner. Therefore, if you have a heart that actively gives glory to Him, there is no need to fear that God will compel His glory from you in a passive way.

Thirdly, if you have a heart that trembles at the Word, know that God has a special intention for you in that very word of salvation. Whenever God brings a message of life and salvation to any congregation, He has a specific aim at your soul. He directs His words of life and salvation towards you. Consider the Scripture in Acts 13:16: "Men of Israel, and you who fear God, listen." But pay attention to what is said in verse 26: "Brothers, children of the family of Abraham, and those among you who fear God, to us has been sent the message of this salvation." If there is a soul that fears the Lord, that trembles in His presence, the word of salvation is sent to that soul. Whenever you come to hear anything about life and salvation in the preaching of the Word, know that God has you in mind specifically. The word of this salvation is sent to you.

Fourthly, if you tremble at God's Word, you shall be comforted. The Word of God contains just as much material to bring comfort to a soul as it does to make it tremble and fear. For this, I could provide you with many promises from Scripture. Let's consider these three.

The first promise is found a verse or two after my text, which I have also mentioned before: "Hear the word of the Lord, you who tremble at his word. Your brothers who hate you and exclude you because of my name have said, 'Let the Lord be glorified, that we may see your joy!' But they will be put to shame." It's as if God is saying, "You trembled, so much so that you didn't dare do as others did, especially in matters of worship. You didn't venture as they did, and as a result, they cast you out. But here is a promise for you: The Lord will appear to bring you joy, and they will be ashamed." The Lord has fulfilled this promise many times.

Another promise is found in Proverbs 13:13: "Whoever despises the word will be destroyed, but whoever fears the commandment will be rewarded." God will reward you for this. Do you come before the Lord with a heart that trembles at his word? When you hear his word, do you receive it with a trembling heart? The one who fears the commandment will be rewarded. This promise is the opposite of the earlier threat.

And a third promise is found in Isaiah 50:10: "Who among you fears the Lord and obeys the word of his servant? Let the one who walks in the dark, who has no light, trust in the name of the Lord and rely on their God." This is for the soul that has such a trembling disposition of heart that it dares not disobey God's voice in his word. Perhaps there is someone here who sits in darkness and cannot see any light, who has walked with a trembling heart in response to God's word, and can appeal to God, saying, "Lord, you know all things. You know that I wouldn't disobey your voice for anything in the world. My heart stands in awe of your word." Yet, perhaps this soul is currently in darkness and sees no light. To such a soul, the Lord looks and speaks, saying, "Let that soul trust in the name of the Lord and rely on their God," for there is true mercy for such a soul. This is the fourth stream of consolation for those who tremble at the word of God, that this word of God will certainly bring them comfort.

Fifthly, another source of comfort is that this disposition of your heart, trembling at God's word, is accepted in place of obedience. Even if you cannot obey God's word as you would like, the Lord will spare you. The soul that recognizes its many weaknesses and is unable to fully obey the truths revealed in the word, yet trembles at it, shall find peace. I say the Lord accepts this trembling disposition instead of obedience, and indeed, even more so. The act of obedience itself does not hold as much significance as this; for a hypocrite can perform the act of obedience, but they lack this trembling. In Malachi 3:16, it is clearly referring to such a disposition, for in verse 15, it says, "And now we call the proud happy; yes, those who work wickedness are raised up; yes, those who tempt God are even delivered." But in verse 16, "Then those who feared the Lord spoke with one another. The Lord paid attention and heard them, and a book of remembrance was written before him of those who feared the Lord and esteemed his name." Notice how God loves to emphasize this and savor it, as we do with things that are sweet. He does not merely say "for them," but "for those who feared the Lord and esteemed his name." And the text continues, "They shall be mine, says the Lord of hosts, in the day when I make up my treasured possession, and I will spare them as a man spares his son who serves him." Therefore, God does not say, "To him will I look who does my word," but "to him who trembles at my word." A learned person commenting on this passage said, "There is more godliness in the trembling of the heart than in the work of the hand." God accepts it, and therefore be comforted in this.

Sixthly, another stream of comfort is that the Lord will reveal himself to this soul. Among all the dispositions in the world, the Lord loves to manifest himself to someone like this. Though it may not happen immediately, wait upon him, and the Lord will make known the most glorious things to you. You will come to know the mind of God more than anyone else. I will provide you with a significant text to support this idea: those who have trembling hearts at God's word come to know the mind of God sooner than anyone else in the world. The text can be found in Ezra 10:3. It says, "Now therefore let us make a covenant with our God to put away all these wives and their children, according to the counsel of my lord and of those who tremble at the commandment of our God. Let it be done according to the Law." The speaker urges them to act according to the counsel of his lord and those who tremble at the commandment of God.

As if to say, certainly they understand God's intentions, let's follow their advice, let's heed their counsel. Those who come before God and tremble at His word are the men and women who comprehend the nature of God better than anyone else. It is not said, "Let us do according to the counsel of my Lord and of the wise, learned, and understanding men among us," but rather "of those who tremble at His word." They know the mind of God.

And indeed, my brethren, it is wiser to seek counsel from those who tremble at God's word than from any other people in the world. Learned individuals who possess bold spirits and live licentious and wicked lives do not understand the secrets of God as those who tremble at His word do. There is a gracious promise to this effect in Psalm 25:14: "The secret of the Lord is with those who fear Him, and He will show them His covenant." They shall understand God's secrets. Others may comprehend some outward aspects of God, but only those who fear the Lord have the promise of understanding His secrets and His covenant.

Seventhly, those who fear and tremble at God's word can find comfort. Why? Because the very word that you now tremble at is the word that God will compel the entire world to tremble at one day. God will honour His word before men and angels. Consider, oh, what unimaginable joy it must bring to the heart of a man or woman when God magnifies His word before the entire world. To think, this is the very word in which I saw the dreadful authority of God before when I lived in the world. This is the word that I esteemed and obeyed, and now God has come to fulfill it before men and angels. And now I see those who disregarded it trembling, even though it will be of no benefit to them. Therefore, blessed be God that while I lived, I trembled at His word, and now the Lord has come to magnify it so gloriously before men and angels.

Rest assured that there is a time coming when the Lord will bring honour to His word before the entire world. Therefore, those who currently tremble in reverence of it are truly blessed. Surely, their hearts will be filled with comfort when God comes and bestows honour upon His word in the presence of all.

Fifthly, once again, if this is the disposition that the Lord values so greatly, allow me, my brethren, to speak a word of rebuke to those who are far from possessing such a heart. Indeed, God looks for those who tremble at His word. But where does God find objects to behold? Even now, God is looking upon this great congregation, seeking to find one who trembles at His word. However, Lord, though we hope that You have some objects to behold, how many souls do You sometimes gaze upon before finding such an object? Oh, no! It is the word that the angels long to understand. It is the word that thousands of souls in heaven bless the name of God for knowing, yet you disregard it as if it were worthless.

There is another group even further away, and they are those who take the liberty to argue against the word as if it were their equal. It is enough that you argue among your equals, but understand that even though the person speaking it may be your equal, the word of God is above you. In James 4, it is said, "If you judge the law, you are not a doer of the law but a judge." These individuals do not come to be doers of the law, but to be judges of the law.

Certainly, if God were to humble the hearts of men, they would not have so many objections against the truths of God that are proclaimed. But observe how God addresses them in His word, they will be inclined to turn their accusations towards their own hearts. There is a significant scripture that illustrates this, especially when compared with another passage. The first is found in Job 38:2, where God speaks to Job, whose heart had not yet been fully humbled. Now, take note of what happens when God humbles Job in Chapter 42:9. Job responds, as if saying, "Who is the man? Well, it is I." He charges himself, just as God did before. This is a clear indication that the heart has been humbled when objections against the word disappear and the heart is willing to acknowledge the same charges brought forth by the word.

Thirdly, those who persistently disobey and rebel against the Word of God are to be rebuked. You know that your ways are contrary to what you hear in the Word, yet you continue without hesitation. Oh, how audacious is your heart to presume to persist in ways that you know are against God's Word! What do you expect to gain? Do you not fear the consequences described in God's Word? Do you not consider the risk of forfeiting all the good that is revealed there? Are you willing, or do you dare to endure the full extent of the evil threatened in the Word? Isn't it the Word that can save your soul if you are to be saved? Let me pose this question to all of you who boldly persist in sin despite what you hear revealed in the Word: Do you actually expect to be saved by God's Word, yes or no? "Receive with meekness the implanted word which is able to save your souls." Can you truly believe that you will be saved by a Word that you persistently rebel against? This is the pride of your heart, that you dare to take such risks. Consider the Scripture in Jeremiah 13:15, "Hear and give ear; be not proud, for the Lord has spoken." So I say to those who continue in a constant state of rebellion against the Word, "Hear and give ear." Do not merely listen and let it pass by. Do not be proud, for the Lord has spoken. When you hear and refuse to heed what is said, but instead persist in rebellion against the truth that is revealed, it is a clear sign of your proud heart. The Lord has spoken, and it is only fitting for the creature to yield and submit.

Fourthly, there are others who not only live contrary to the Word, but they are also under the condemning sentence of God's Word. They come and hear God's Word condemning them for their sins, and their consciences confirm that they are indeed guilty of the sins that God's Word condemns. Yet, they can sit there unaffected, numb, and with hardened hearts. This is not trembling at God's Word. It is even more significant for a single sentence from God's Word to condemn a sinner than if all the angels in heaven and all people on earth were to pronounce a sentence of condemnation. And yet, some of you can sit day after day under the condemning sentences of God's Word, as if God's Word is true, and you are a condemned soul in the present moment.

I have no doubt that there are many who come to hear the Word and inwardly conclude, "If this is true, I am in a wretched state. I am condemned if that is true."

I remember knowing a man once who engaged in wrongdoing with another person, yet they both attended sermons together. Afterwards, he would say to the other person, "Madam, if what the minister speaks is true, you and I are in a dire condition." Similarly, many people say, "If it is true, I am a profoundly miserable person." Let me ask each and every one of you in this congregation a question: Suppose that all the threats in God's Word are true and are indeed the Word of God, and suppose that they must all be fulfilled. What would you think of your condition then? I have no doubt that many consciences would answer, "Certainly, my condition would be utterly unbearable if this is true. But I hope things will not turn out so dire."

Well then, it all comes down to this: The foundation of your peace, present rest, and comfort relies on your hope that things will not turn out as bad as they are revealed in the Word. Is this not the basis of your soul's rest and comfort?

And if you were certain that things would indeed be as bad as they are proclaimed to be, you would say to yourself, "I will never continue in my wicked ways again. I would never be able to sleep peacefully at night." Therefore, if those things were true, you would be unable to sleep. Now, I say, cursed be that peace, that comfort, that sleep, that state which has no foundation except the hope that God's Word is not true. But this is the sole basis for the comforts that many people rely on throughout their lives. I am afraid that if God were to call upon individuals and ask them, "What is the foundation of your entire life?" they would be forced to say, "Lord, it is based on the hope that things are not as bad as ministers preach from the Word." Now I declare, cursed be that hope that is grounded on no other basis. Take a look at yourself. You have a bold heart that dares to risk your soul and eternal destiny on such a hope. If God's Word proves true, you will be a lost and doomed creature for all eternity. Yet, you dare to take such a risk! It is a bold venture. Oh, consider this, all of you who can sit under the condemning power of God's Word without having your hearts deeply affected. Learn to tremble at it.

Fifthly, there is another group of people who need to be rebuked on this matter. These are the individuals whose hearts rise up against God's Word. They do not tremble at it. When the Word of God pierces their consciences and instills fear, their only desire and effort is to remove it from their hearts. They wish they had not attended the sermon. They are troubled by it and seek the company of the wicked to rid themselves of the fear of God's Word. These people are far from trembling. Oh, poor creature that you are, how much better it would be for you to pursue the work of God that may benefit your soul. In the future, you may find yourself regretting your foolishness. You will have reason to say, "What a blessed thing it would have been if I had continued in the work of God that He began in me at that time."

Sixthly, there is another group who rage against the Word of God, just as we read about the wicked King Jehoiakim in Jeremiah 36. When the scroll was brought before him and read, he took a pen-knife and cut it, throwing it into the fire. I once knew someone who, while reading the scripture against adultery, tore out the pages. But consider this: Jehoiakim's father's heart melted when the Word was read, while his own son took a pen-knife and cut it, tossing it into the fire. This was such a great evil that I have read that the Jews observed a yearly fast to mourn this sin of their king.

Seventhly, how far removed are those who scorn at God's Word from trembling! For instance, when Christ Himself preached against covetousness in Luke 16, those who were covetous derided Him. Similarly, in various scriptures, I could show the contempt and scorn that people directed towards Isaiah and Paul for the word they delivered. However, I will not elaborate further to avoid prolonging my discourse. Oh, this is also an immensely dreadful wickedness for anyone to be guilty of such a height of impiety, as the Lord expects trembling at His Word while they choose to scorn it.

Eighthly, there is another group, although not as severe, who jest at God's Word. But beware, my brethren, of treating Scripture as a source of jests. Wise men should never jest about two things: those in misery and holy things. So when you engage with God's Word and make jests out of Scripture, you are meddling with sharp tools. Know that it is a serious form of taking God's name in vain for anyone to mock Scripture. I recall a statement by Luther: if a person wants to play and jest, let them jest with their children, with their toys. But as soon as they come to hear the Word, they should obey without any dispute. They may jest with other things, but not with that. In another instance, Luther said that it is not a matter of play to hear God's Word. When the Word touches the soul, it is like thunder that can topple the mightiest things by its power. Hearing the Word is not a matter of jesting, but of trembling. So who are you to mock the Word, object to it, rebel against it, or argue with it? Who are you to obscure knowledge like this? What are you that you can raise your heart against the blessed Word of God? The Word of the Lord shakes the heavens and the earth (Psalm 104:32). God merely looks upon the earth and it trembles. Yet God speaks to you and you refuse to tremble. In Job 26:11, it is said that the pillars of heaven tremble and are astonished at God's reproof. Pay attention to the text. If

God merely reproves, the pillars of heaven are astonished. How many times has God reproved you through His Word and you have not trembled?

God reproves you for your Sabbath-breaking, swearing, keeping bad company, neglecting His worship in your family, and your atheism. In Job 9:6, it is said that the shaking of the earth causes the pillars to tremble. The pillars of the earth and the pillars of heaven tremble. Who are you to stand before the Word of God? Even holy men tremble when they hear the Word. In Jeremiah 23:9, it is written, "My heart is broken within me; all my bones shake. I am like a drunken man, like a man overcome by wine, because of the Lord and His holy words." The saints tremble, as stated in Habakkuk 3:16, "When I heard, my belly trembled; my lips quivered at the voice." Even the angels in heaven listen with reverence to the Word of the Lord. They do His commandments and heed the voice of His word. They approach God's Word with respect and obedience. And you, what are you doing all this time? When God speaks, the pillars of the earth and heaven tremble. The saints of God tremble, the holy prophets tremble. Even the angels tremble. Yet you stand before God's Word without a trembling heart. Let me speak these two or three things to you.

First, know that the Lord cannot help but look upon one who trembles at His Word with acceptance. But it is impossible for Him not to despise and detest a hard, stony heart like yours. You are a poor, vile wretch whom the smallest word from my mouth could send to the depths of hell. Yet when I speak, you pay no attention. It is impossible for the Lord to look upon you without bringing destruction. Especially if you are filled with base fears. When your master or someone in authority speaks, you fear them. But when the infinite, eternal, and dreadful God speaks, you do not fear. Know that the Word you do not fear is working your destruction. God will work fear into your heart, and one day you will tremble. As written in Isaiah 51:17, "Awake, awake, stand up, O Jerusalem, you who have drunk from the hand of the Lord the cup of His fury; you have drunk the dregs of the cup of trembling, and drained it." There will come a time when God will make sinners who do not tremble at His Word drink the dregs of the cup of trembling. The dregs may become your portion.

Furthermore, when God causes trembling, it's possible that He will pay as little attention to your fears as you pay to His Word. That passage in Proverbs 1 is most dreadful: "I will laugh at your calamity; I will mock when your fear cometh."

In conclusion, I exhort all of us to strive for such a blessed disposition of the heart. In Hosea 13:1 and 5, it is mentioned that when Ephraim spoke, trembling would ensue. Some interpretations suggest that this was to the honour of Ephraim, as when Ephraim spoke, the people around him trembled.

Surely, it must be an honour to the great God that when He speaks, all people should tremble. The voice of the Lord is full of majesty and glory, and thus it is fitting for us all to tremble before Him. Let us ponder upon the weightiness of His word and consider the majesty of God that is revealed within it.

Consider this: God has consistently fulfilled His word throughout time. The word of God has overwhelmed countless souls, casting them down and leading them to eternal ruin by the power of His word. Therefore, it is only fitting that I should tremble.

I implore you to pray to God that He may reveal to your soul the glory of His name found within His word. In Deuteronomy, the Lord speaks of giving the people a trembling heart as a curse, but you should beseech it from God as a blessing.

And you should demonstrate that God has instilled this disposition in your hearts through attentive reverence, just as fear causes the eyes to be focused. If men and women truly trembled at the Word, they would not be indifferent or sleep through it, but rather they would pay close attention. Oh, may the Lord continue to inspire awe for His Word in your hearts.

You may argue that if the Word were spoken directly from heaven, then you would surely pay heed, but as it is, you cannot.

There were several things I intended to discuss regarding this matter, but I will only give you one Scripture to counter that objection so that it will no longer prevail. In 2 Chronicles, the last verse of the chapter, it is stated: "And he did what was evil in the sight of the Lord his God and did not humble himself before Jeremiah the prophet, who spoke from the mouth of the Lord." The Lord charges Zedekiah with doing evil before Him and not humbling himself before Jeremiah the prophet. Now, Jeremiah was a humble man, what significance did he hold in comparison to King Zedekiah? But still, Zedekiah did not humble himself before Jeremiah the prophet, who spoke from the mouth of the Lord. Therefore, do not say that you would tremble only if God spoke from heaven. Instead, when we speak according to God's Word, God expects you to humble your souls before the great God through the ministry of His Word that we bring to you.

Therefore, as you demonstrate through your attentive presence that you recognize the authority, also demonstrate it through obedience and the reformation of your lives and conduct. Let your reformation be evidence that the authority of God's Word is indeed working in your hearts.

Tremble before it in this manner so that the Word may be honoured and your souls may find comfort, leading to eternal salvation.

# Chapter Four

## SERMON IV

## But by Way of Application.

"Because thine heart was tender, and thou hast humbled thyself before the Lord, when thou heardest what I spake against this place, and against the inhabitants thereof, that they should become a desolation and a curse, and hast rent thy clothes, and wept before me; I also have heard thee, saith the Lord." 2 Kings 22:19

There are two gracious dispositions of the soul by which the name of God is sanctified in the hearing of His Word. The first is a trembling heart, which we discussed last time, and we have chosen this text to address the second.

The words that have been read to you are a part of the famous story that shows how Josiah, a gracious and godly king, was affected upon hearing God's Word. He was deeply moved upon hearing of God's displeasure, both against himself and the people. The essence of the story is this: In the eighteenth year of his reign, there was great concern for the repair of the Temple of the Lord. During the restoration work, the Book of the Law was discovered, which they had not seen for a long time. It was read in the presence of King Josiah, and upon hearing the words of the book, his heart immediately melted, and he became greatly troubled. He could not find peace until he sought further understanding of God's intentions regarding what was written in that book. He sent a message to the prophetess Huldah to inquire about God's will. Huldah gave him a response that pertained to both the people and the king. The words that have been read to you are specifically the part of God's answer concerning the king, stating, "Because your heart was tender, and you humbled yourself, etc. Therefore, I have heard you," declares the Lord, "and you shall die in peace." In this story, there are four important questions that help us to understand it better.

The first question is: What is this Book of the Law that was read to Josiah?

Secondly, why did he send to Huldah instead of Jeremiah the prophet, who was active during that time?

Thirdly, what is the reason behind the severe response from the Lord through Huldah against the people, even though they were on a hopeful path of reformation?

And fourthly, we come to the fulfillment of God's promise to Josiah that he would die in peace, as mentioned later in the chapter. However, if you continue reading the story, you will find that Josiah died in a war. I will briefly address these four points to shed some light on the history before we delve into the words that were read.

First, regarding the book that was found, the text clearly states that it was the Book of the Law. It is strange that the Book of the Law was not available to the people of the Jews and that they had not possessed it until now. It is one of the most remarkable occurrences mentioned in the Scriptures, that it was considered a wondrous thing to find the Book of the Law during Josiah's time. There is much debate among interpreters regarding this matter. Some suggest that the book was burned during the time of Ahaz, who destroyed all the copies he could find to prevent them from testifying against his departure from the true religion. It has been the way of wicked rulers to burn Scriptures, such as Diocletian's attempt to destroy as many copies of Scripture as possible. However, God has miraculously preserved the Scriptures to this day. No book has faced as much opposition and deliberate destruction as the Scriptures, and yet God has preserved it above all other books. It is the oldest book in the world, written long before any other extant book, and yet it has been fiercely opposed. This serves as strong evidence that God acknowledges its significance.

However, it is unlikely that the copy was burnt during Ahaz's reign, and that they did not have access to it, because between these two reigns, there was the righteous reign of Hezekiah. It appears that during Ahaz's time, many copies were indeed burned, so they had only a few during Hezekiah's reign. Then came Manasseh after Hezekiah, who was a wicked king and reigned for fifty-five years. It is likely that throughout his reign, he continued in wickedness, opposing God and all godliness. His son, Ammon, who succeeded him, was equally wicked. Therefore, during the reigns of these two evil kings, there were probably very few copies of the Book of the Law to be found.

Chrysostom, in his sermon on Matthew and Corinthians, believed it was only the Book of Deuteronomy. Many others also believe that it was at least some portion of the Law that was not available at that time, specifically the 27th and 28th chapters of Deuteronomy, which were read before Josiah and deeply moved his heart.

By the way, we can learn from this how blessed we are to have not only the Book of the Law but also the Gospel, the Prophets, the histories of the kings and judges, the Psalms, the Epistles, and the book of Revelation. We have all these books in our homes that we can read constantly. In Josiah's time, it was a remarkable thing to have certain portions of the Book of the Law read, especially before the king.

Secondly, when Josiah heard this book being read, particularly those chapters, his heart was deeply affected. He realized that he had been living in sin against God, even though he was ignorant of it. He understood that ignorance would not excuse him. Before this, he did not comprehend the danger of the sins he and his people had been committing. But as soon as he became aware of their sins and the impending danger, his heart was greatly troubled.

This teaches us that we should not think our ignorance excuses us from our sins. As soon as God brings His Word among us to reveal the danger of our sins, God expects our hearts to be humbled before Him for our transgressions.

Josiah was so humbled that he couldn't find rest. A heart that truly understands the evil of sin cannot be at peace until it knows more about God's intentions. It will seek diligently to learn God's mind regarding it. How can I sleep peacefully when I perceive that God's wrath is against me? I need to know whether God is reconciled to me or not. This was Josiah's situation.

Now, let's address the second question. Why did Josiah send to Huldah instead of Jeremiah? After all, Jeremiah was a renowned prophet in Israel at the same time. It is true that Jeremiah began his prophecy in the thirteenth year of Josiah.

Therefore, some suggest this reason: Jeremiah was a young prophet. He began his prophecy in the thirteenth year of Josiah, and at that time, he had only been in ministry for five years. Jeremiah even refers to himself as a child who cannot speak. So, they think that Josiah may have considered it more suitable to send to Huldah, who had more experience, even though she was a woman. However, I don't think that was the reason for not sending to Jeremiah. It is more likely that Jeremiah was not as accessible as Huldah. He lived in Anathoth, not in Jerusalem, and it is possible that he was not present. The good king was so eager to know God's mind that he was willing to receive the message from anyone, regardless of their status, as long as he could learn what God's mind was.

Now, let's move on to the third question. It is quite noteworthy in the response given by the prophet to the messengers sent by King Josiah. The Lord says, "Behold, I will bring evil upon this place and upon its inhabitants, all the words of the book which the King of Judah has read." It is a peculiar response. Wasn't the country in a good and hopeful state of reformation, with the king's heart melting and him weeping upon realizing God's displeasure for their sins, sins of which he was already convinced? As soon as he became aware, he started weeping and had a strong desire to know God's mind. Weren't they now in a highly promising condition for reformation? Despite all this, the response states that God will bring upon this place and its inhabitants all the words of the book that the King of Judah has read. This reveals a somber lesson for us.

A people may find themselves in a situation where all the reformation and repentance in the world cannot protect them from temporal afflictions inflicted by God. If you continue reading the chapter, you will discover a significant reformation, and yet all the words of the book must be fulfilled.

This shows us the power of sin. It can create such a division between God and us that, no matter what we do, we may still experience temporal afflictions in this world. We can see an example in the case of Moses, whose repentance could not prevent him from being cut off before reaching the land of Canaan. The Lord did not grant Moses' request. Though undoubtedly Moses repented for the sin that provoked God, he was not allowed to enter Canaan. However, since the Lord has not specifically revealed such judgments for people in the present time, we should not assume this applies to us. Instead, we must take this lesson seriously, not to play around or trifle with God, lest a decree be issued against us with no way to avoid it.

Now, regarding the fourth question, there appears to be a difficulty in the answer the Lord gave regarding Josiah. The Lord promised him mercy and that he would die in peace. However, as we later learn in the story, Josiah was killed in battle. How can this be reconciled with the promise that he would die in peace?

The answer to that is commonly understood as follows: Josiah died in peace because he had made peace with God. His sins were forgiven, and there was peace between God and his soul. Therefore, regardless of the circumstances of his death, if there is peace between a person and God, they die in peace. Even amidst storms and turmoil in the world, as long as there is peace between God and their soul, they die in peace.

But I believe there is much more to it than that. We must provide a further explanation to make the Word of God true, and that is, Josiah died in peace, specifically in the sense of the peace of the kingdom. In fact, that was peace to him. The war in which he died did not pose a threat to the kingdom. As you can read in the subsequent part of the story, when he went to war, the kingdom did not suffer the dreadful evils that were previously threatened. Before Judah was carried into captivity, the Lord took Josiah away. So when he died, he left the kingdom in a good state at that time, and he left God's ordinances among them. Thus, his death was considered peaceful in relation to the kingdom. This interpretation seems to be supported in 2 Chronicles 38:28, where the story is repeated, stating that Josiah would be gathered to his fathers in peace, and his eyes would not witness the subsequent evils that would befall the kingdom and its inhabitants. Therefore, he was gathered to his fathers in peace because he did not witness the future calamities that would befall his kingdom.

In truth, regardless of how a person dies, if the kingdom and the church where they live are in peace, enjoying their freedoms and God's ordinances, it can be said that they died in peace. It brings me peace knowing that I am leaving the church and the kingdom in a state of peace.

Especially knowing that not long after, the kingdom would experience severe distresses, which Josiah died before. He is described as dying in peace because he passed away before those events occurred. However, to shed more light on this remarkable and well-known story, let us now focus on the specific words. The response of the prophetess regarding the king begins in verse 18. She instructs the messengers to convey to the king of Judah, "Because your heart was tender." As for the people, God declares that He will not be entreated for them. He states that they will certainly feel His stroke and all the words written in the book will come upon them.

From this, we can observe that when the Lord is bringing public calamity upon a nation, He makes distinctions. In this case, it is directed "to the king of Judah." Is there anyone with a tender, broken heart, one that is broken over the sins of the nation? God will have His eye on them. It is true that at times, even godly individuals may pass away during times of national judgment, but it is usually because God has a specific purpose to accomplish through their deaths.

But we do not find that God makes such distinctions now, for godly individuals are taken away just like others. Surely, my brethren, this is meant to make us all tremble and not to rely on anything, neither fasting nor prayer, but to wholly depend on the goodness of the Lord to do with us as He pleases. The fact that God does not make such distinctions now is for the sake of some great work that God has yet to reveal to us. However, we can be confident that God will receive as much glory from their deaths as He would have received from their lives. Regardless of the current obscurity of God's ways towards us, there will come a time when God will make distinctions, when the difference between those who fear God and those who do not will be known.

There are very few (though they are being pursued for the sins of the nation) who have faith for deliverance from temporal judgments, and that may be one reason. Even though the Lord promises deliverance, He desires our faith to extend to that promise, to fully entrust our souls to it more than we currently do. However, it is challenging for anyone to have such faith to confidently and definitively conclude that they will be delivered from temporal affliction. We are to marvel at God's dispensations in this matter and wait for further revelation of His intentions towards us. Nevertheless, He makes distinctions regarding the king of Judah.

Oh, it is fitting for the greatest ones in the world, kings and princes, that when God threatens, their hearts should melt before Him. No one is too great to humble themselves before the great God. It is true that we have a wretched generation of men who, many times, while they may tremble and shake at the threats of their superiors, think themselves good enough to sin against the Lord and resist His Word. But Josiah did not do so.

But you may argue, "Perhaps he was just a child?" No, he was a king in his full vigour and strength; he was twenty-six years old. And that age is the peak of vitality, especially for courtiers and great men. Yet, King Josiah, at the age of twenty-six, amidst his nobles, though he was not visibly in any immediate danger, humbled himself and wept before the Lord upon hearing His word. Therefore, this is the response from God concerning him: "Because your heart was tender, I have accepted you, and you shall have peace."

So, in these words, there are four significant aspects to consider:

- What influenced Josiah's heart? What were the reasons for his heart becoming tender?

- The state and disposition of Josiah's heart—it melted.

- The outcome of this:

a) He humbled himself.

b) He tore his clothes.

c) He wept before the Lord.

- Lastly, God's gracious acceptance of this, as He declares, "I have also heard you," says the Lord.

I will not discuss Josiah's disposition in this melting state at this time. I will only touch upon a point or two regarding the occasion of this, as stated in the text: "Your heart was tender, and you have humbled yourself before the Lord when you heard what I spoke against the inhabitants, etc."

How did he hear it?

Through Shaphan the scribe, who brought a few old, torn, and rotten papers, presumably found hidden in a hole of the temple wall amidst the rubble for many years. It is likely that these were very old papers. They were presented before the king and read aloud. The text tells us that Josiah's heart was tender, and he humbled himself upon hearing what God spoke. God did not speak to him through a prophet or from heaven. If God had spoken audibly from heaven, disclosing the sins of his court and kingdom, it would have been a significant event for his heart to melt. Or if the Lord had raised up an extraordinary prophet to denounce dreadful threats against him, it would have been something noteworthy. However, it was simply upon hearing a few papers that had been discovered among the temple rubble. From this, we can make two observations:

Firstly, when the Lord desires to humble a soul, He can do it with minimal effort.

Secondly, it is highly pleasing to God when people immediately relent, yield, and humble themselves upon hearing His displeasure declared against them. These are the two observations derived from the cause of Josiah's disposition.

The first point is truly wonderful and remarkable: when God decides to work on the heart of a sinner, even a small matter can make their heart relent and yield to God. Some people resist it fiercely, while others yield at the slightest prompting. What a difference there is between Josiah and Pharaoh—both kings! God sends an extraordinary messenger to Pharaoh, who comes in God's name and performs miraculous signs before him, signs that no one else in his nation could replicate. In addition to the miracles, God brings upon the entire kingdom and Pharaoh himself fearful judgments that would send shivers down one's spine just to hear about them. Ten successive judgments, and yet Pharaoh's heart remains hardened. On the other hand, Josiah merely hears a little from some old papers, and his heart immediately yields. When God works, the means are not of great importance; they can be small, weak, and poor, and yet the heart will be led to yield to God in a gracious and holy manner. We read in 1 Kings chapter 19, verse 20, a very notable story. Elijah departs and finds Elisha, the son of Shaphat, plowing with twelve yoke of oxen before him. Elijah passes by and casts his mantle upon him—that's all he did. Now, Elisha held a prominent position, even though he was at the plow. The twelve yoke of oxen belonged to him. Elijah simply cast his mantle upon Elisha, and the text says that Elisha left the oxen and ran after Elijah, saying, "Let me kiss my father and mother, and then I will follow you." Elijah responds, "Go back again, for what have I done to you?" But there was a hidden power that accompanied the casting of Elijah's mantle upon Elisha, and his heart was drawn to him, so that nothing could hinder him from joining Elijah. Therefore, when the appointed time of the Lord comes to win the heart of a man or woman, even the tiniest thing in the world can accomplish it. They will yield immediately.

It's just like the situation with Peter in Luke 22:61. Peter had sinned greatly against Christ, and the text says that when Christ looked at him, Peter went out and wept bitterly. He threw himself out, that's the meaning of the word, with a kind of force, he had had enough of it. The Lord Christ only gave him a look, and he went and wept bitterly. Oh, there are many to whom the Lord Christ speaks over and over again, and their hearts remain unaffected. But when the Lord decides to work on the heart, it only takes God giving a look to a soul.

Perhaps some of you who are continuing in sinful ways have heard many warnings against them, yet your hearts remain unmoved. But if the Lord's appointed time has come, it's just one look upon you, and your eyes are opened to have a glimpse of the God you have sinned against, and the transformation is accomplished. In Song of Solomon 5:4, the Church says, "My beloved put in his hand by the hole of the door, and my bowels were moved for him." The Church, being complacent, presents arguments against going out to Christ, saying, "I have taken off my coat, how can I put it on again? I have washed my feet, how can I defile them?"

Oh, it would be so troublesome, and she was reluctant to face any trouble. But pay attention to the fourth verse: "My beloved put in his hand by the hole of the door, and my heart was moved." Why was that more significant than knocking? Because he had knocked before, but the time had not come. It may be the same with many souls. The Lord may stand knocking at the door of your soul again and again, over time, and yet you may have one excuse or another to put Him off. But when God's appointed time arrives, He only needs to touch your heart once, and it's done. A little effort will accomplish it when God's time has come. In Isaiah 11:6, it is prophesied about the times of the Gospel that people will be so receptive to the truths of God that even a child will be able to lead them. Any truth of God delivered by the humblest, weakest, or even a child will lead them.

And this is very prominent in Isaiah 30:21: "And thine ears shall hear a word behind thee, saying, This is the way, walk ye in it, when ye turn to the right hand, and when ye turn to the left." What follows is, "Ye shall defile also the covering of thy graven images of silver, and the ornament of thy molten images of gold, thou shalt cast them away as a menstrual cloth, thou shalt say unto it, Get thee hence." This people were deeply engrossed in their idolatry, and the Prophet found it extremely challenging to turn their hearts away from their idolatrous ways. But now the Lord promises a time when they would simply hear a word, even from

But do not be discouraged, for he may eventually succeed, and God may bless many things that come from him. Therefore, I encourage those who are tasked with addressing such an audience to heed the words of Ecclesiastes 11:6: "In the morning sow your seed, and in the evening do not withhold your hand, for you do not know which will prosper, whether this or that, or whether both alike will be good."

Therefore, let ministers continue to sow their seed and preach persistently. Even if what they have spoken seems as though they were presenting arguments that could move the heart of a devil, or revealing the wretched condition of mankind and the richness of Jesus Christ, they must not be discouraged. They should sow their seed in the morning and not withhold their hand in the evening. They should keep preaching, presenting the Word of God before the hearts of people. Even if it did not have an effect at one time, it may work at another time. Yes, even if they grow weaker and weaker, the Lord can still use them for good, even in their weakest state. In 2 Timothy 2:25, the apostle Paul says to Timothy, "In meekness instructing those that oppose themselves, if God perhaps will give them repentance." Perhaps on a given day, a truth may be imparted from God to a soul, perhaps from this passage or that passage, and the soul may be drawn in.

Use of Encouragement: Another use shall be for the purpose of encouragement for those who feel their hearts being moved by little means. When God hints a truth to you while reading a chapter, during conversations, especially when you gather to hear the Word, and you receive only fragments of God's Word, yet they have a powerful impact on your heart. Are there any such individuals here? Take courage, for the Lord accepts this disposition. Therefore, for your comfort, know that the Lord,

Firstly, this is a sign of a very childlike disposition in you. Just as a father is pleased when he merely raises his finger and the child immediately falls to their knees, a slave may fall down if you approach them with blows, but a child responds to even the slightest look. In Proverbs 17:10, it is stated, "A rebuke goes deeper into a wise man than a hundred blows into a fool." Those who are fools and have base and servile dispositions cannot be influenced by any means.

However, someone with an ingenuous disposition is affected by a word. And if you find that your heart is so tender that a word has an impact on you, this is a sign of the wisdom of God within your soul.

Furthermore, know that it is a sign that God is in His word and that He accompanies what is said to you. It is a comforting thought to realize that, thanks to God, when I hear His word, even the smallest thing reaches my heart. And if you find that your heart is of this nature, where almost everything said sticks with you, you can take comfort in knowing that the Lord does not distance Himself from you in His word.

Thirdly, you can certainly find comfort in the fact that you cannot stray far from God. Why? Because if something small can have an impact on you, then you must be influenced every day. If you have a tender heart and are affected by the smallest things, there is no need to fear that you will ever stray far from God. Souls with stubborn and obstinate hearts go far away from God. The prophet says, "Hearken to me, you who are stubborn-hearted, who are far from righteousness." Stubborn hearts are far from righteousness. However, those with yielding hearts need never fear going far from righteousness. A person with a stubborn spirit may unknowingly drift far from God, but someone with a yielding disposition never needs to fear straying too far from God. Indeed, I may stumble daily like others, but I have this hope that I will never go far from God.

Fourthly, does your heart yield to God upon a little? Take comfort, for the Lord has great things to reveal to your soul. The Lord will disclose great things to the soul that is moved by the smallest matters. A notable example of this is found in John 1:49 and following. You are familiar with what Christ said to Nathaniel, "Do you believe because I told you I saw you under the fig tree? You will see greater things than these." In the same way, I say to your heart, does your heart soften and submit to God upon hearing even the slightest revelation? Take comfort, oh soul! You are a soul for whom the Lord intends to do great things and reveal profound truths. "The secret of the Lord is with those who fear Him, and He will show them His covenant." If there is a soul that fears God and is affected by everything, the secret of the Lord is with that soul, and the Lord will reveal His covenant to that soul.

Treasure this disposition of your heart, and when you see others with hard and stubborn hearts, bless God who has given you such a heart that only requires a little to respond.

# Chapter Five

# SERMON V

## Use

*"Because thine heart was tender"* - 2 Kings 22:19

There are a couple of remaining uses of the point, and then we will briefly move on to the other, so that we can make some progress towards the main point in the text.

Use: When God's time comes, a little will work upon the heart. Now, here is a rebuke to the stubbornness of the hearts of most people who resist even great influences; it is not just a hint of something that will affect them. How many can be rebuked from this? I say, those who have resisted great efforts to impact them. Perhaps many of you have had godly parents who have laboured with all their power to show you the evil of your ways. They have offered admonitions, counsel, and exhortations, but none of it has worked. Maybe you have been in other households where you could have found encouragement, but that has done nothing for you. You have been exposed to powerful preaching, hearing messages that could have made even a devil tremble. You have heard the terrors of the law, but they have had no effect. Moreover, you have heard about the heart-melting mercies of Christ that could have softened even the hardest heart, yet they have not worked on you. God's providence has been at work in your life; you have faced chastisement from God, but that has not impacted you. You have received countless mercies, yet they have not moved you. Conscience itself has been set upon you, terrifying you and bringing you before the judgment seat of God, pleading against you for your sins, but it has done nothing. Despite all these means, you continue to be like a rock in the midst of flowing water—while the water passes by, the rock remains unmoved. Oh, how far is your heart from the heart of King Josiah, who upon hearing a few old papers had his heart immediately melted before the Lord and humbled himself. Well, for you whose hearts are so resistant that it takes so much effort to impact them, know that,

First, know that those things which have not had any impact on you are the very things for which many in heaven are now blessing God. They have experienced the good of them, while you have attended to the Word and it has passed by you without touching your heart. But there are many in heaven who are grateful that they were hearing the Word at that time, even if you did not benefit from it.

Understand that this disposition, where one means must be used after another to reach your heart, is wearisome to the Spirit of God. We know how tiresome it is for us, especially when we speak to people for their own good and they refuse to be persuaded. Realize that you have a heart with a disposition that is burdensome to God. When God speaks to you for your own good, so much effort and commotion are required before anything can have an effect on you. And then, know this:

Secondly, it is a dangerous sign of being reprobate if abundant means do not impact you. You are far from the disposition of the person described in the text. A famous passage regarding this is found in Jeremiah 6:29-30. It speaks of bellows being burnt and lead being consumed by fire, while the refiner's attempts are in vain because the wicked are not removed. They are likened to silver that the refiner desires to melt and purify, but despite blowing the bellows and intensifying the fire, the lead is consumed and no progress is made. The refiner's efforts are in vain. Their hearts are compared to the type of metal that refuses to melt. As a result, they are called reprobate silver because the Lord has rejected them. Eventually, the Lord rejects hearts like these that require so much effort to work on. Therefore, my brethren, strive to have a disposition of heart where a little will have an impact on you. Remember this text. When we consider the greatness of the God we are dealing with, we must recognize that even the slightest hint of His will should prevail with us, even if it is just a word.

And know, it is a mercy from God that you have even a hint of His will, that you have any word to reveal His mind concerning the good of your soul.

First, God expects you to grasp every hint. Perhaps when a minister casually drops a word that closely concerns your soul, even if it is not the main topic of his preaching, the Lord expects you to seize upon it and not rest until your heart is affected by it. In 1 Kings 20, there is a mention of the servants of Ben-Hadad diligently observing whether anything would come from their master and eagerly catching it. Similarly, when we come to the Word, we should approach the great King of Heaven and Earth for our lives. We should diligently observe whether God speaks anything to our hearts and swiftly seize upon it. Blessed are those whose hearts are moved by even a little. While God may use great means for the good of some, for others, if a little is not enough, they will never be moved.

The next point is about Josiah. When he heard the Book of the Law being read, his heart was immediately turned, unlike Felix who said, "I will hear more about this another time." Josiah yielded right away. From this, the point is clear: It is highly pleasing to God when the souls of people promptly relent, yield, and humble themselves as soon as they hear God's displeasure being expressed against them.

Sometimes, God is pleased to implant a truth in the heart that does not immediately take effect, but remains there for a long time, perhaps for days, weeks, months, or even years. I have known some who were moved by the Word as they were hearing it, but the Lord implanted it in their consciences, and it only took effect when they were on their sickbeds. Similarly, there are admonitions and exhortations given to people that may not stir them immediately, but later on, God may bless them and bring about a response. It is like the seed cast into the ground that does not sprout immediately if a drought follows, but when rain comes, it springs up when you thought it had died. The same applies to the seed of the Word. We sow it, and during a period of prosperity, we may think it has died, but later on, when God sends afflictions, the Word springs up. It is a good thing that the Word of God can work in the hearts of men and women at any time. However, it is more pleasing to God when the heart yields immediately upon the first hearing. This was the case with David. In 2 Samuel 12:12, when the prophet Nathan came to tell David about his sin, David humbled himself before the Lord immediately upon receiving Nathan's message. He did not ask Nathan to leave and consider it later; instead, he confessed, "I have sinned against the Lord." He recognized his wrongdoing and felt deep remorse before the Lord, exclaiming, "What shall I do?"

And so, as we see in Acts 2, while they were listening, their hearts were pricked before they even left the presence of God. The mere sound of the Word was enough to penetrate their hearts. When the Lord is pleased to work in the hearts of His people, His Word has an immediate effect. The Lord can open the heart when He sets the key to it. Many hearts are like rusty locks that require a lot of effort to open, especially if the key is not the right one or if it doesn't fit every ward. However, when the key fits perfectly and every ward is aligned, even a child can turn it with a single finger. Sometimes the Lord speaks His Word in such a way that it fits perfectly into the hearts of those who are like rusty locks. There may be objections and barriers in their hearts, but when the Lord directs His Word to them, the key fits perfectly, and their hearts open instantly. In an instant, the heart of a person who has been closed off to God throughout their life is opened.

There are several reasons why the hearts of people should open and yield to God immediately.

Firstly, it is because of the submission that creatures owe to God. Just as you expect your children to yield to you promptly, it is not enough if they yield to you after many punishments and words. A stubborn child is one who takes a long time to yield. However, when a child yields to you immediately, it pleases you. Likewise, the Lord expects us to yield to Him promptly, without prolonging our resistance or requiring many arguments and admonitions. We should come in and yield to Him without delay.

Secondly, yielding to God immediately prevents a great deal of evil. When a person promptly yields to God, it prevents them from engaging in numerous sins. Even if the Lord, in His infinite mercy, eventually converts those who have resisted Him, one must reflect on the abundance of evil committed during the time of resistance. If one looks back at their past, they may realise that God had been stirring their hearts before. They may ask themselves, "Didn't I hear the word of the Lord before? How much better it would have been if I had yielded to Him from the beginning!" By resisting, one has allowed a multitude of sins to accumulate since that time.

I should have explained what it is in God's word that causes a soul to yield to Him immediately. However, I will briefly move on to the application of this principle.

Application:

Therefore, first and foremost, it can serve as a consolation to those whose hearts have yielded to God immediately. I hope there are some among you whose hearts, like Lydia's, have been receptive to the key of God's word, and upon hearing it for the first time, your hearts surrendered before the Lord. How great a comfort can you find in this! You can honestly declare before the Lord, "It is true, there was a time when I lived in blindness, ignorance, profanity, and ungodliness. But blessed be God, ever since He revealed His will to me, my heart has yielded to Him." Can you say this? Oh, what a blessed thing it would be if many of you could say, "Lord, indeed, in the days of my ignorance, I lived a profane and ungodly life because I didn't know any better. But as soon as You made Your truth known to me, my heart surrendered and yielded to You."

There are many individuals whom God is currently working on, and they are now seeking God's mercy. However, they face the temptation that they have resisted God for so long. This temptation weighs heavily on them, and they would give anything to be free from it. But you have been delivered from such a temptation. Blessed are you who yield immediately to the Word of God. In Revelation 4:1, John describes hearing a voice like a trumpet speaking to him. Then, in the second verse, he says, "Immediately I was in the Spirit, and behold, a throne was set in Heaven..."

Have you ever heard the voice of the Word like a trumpet, and can you say, "Immediately I was in the Spirit" or "Immediately the Spirit was in me"? I say, peace be with you in this matter. For this is highly pleasing to the Lord, and it is a sign of a genuine spirit. And know that the Lord will be as present in the ways of mercy towards you as you are present in hearing Him. If you are immediately moved upon hearing the Word, and I stress the word "immediately," the Lord will be present in His mercy towards you. He will be just as quick to do you good as you are to yield obedience to Him. Therefore, those who have this kind of response can expect comfort sooner than others. Many people remain under the terrors of the law for a long time. Why? Because the Lord deals with them in the same way they dealt with Him. God may have been calling upon you for many years before you hearkened to Him. So, considering that you made God wait for so long and did not come to Him, you may be willing to wait for comfort.

Now, for you young ones, if you come in immediately upon the very first realization of the dangerous condition you are in, I tell you that you may find comfort very soon. The Lord heard at the beginning of Daniel's supplication. The Lord would not delay His mercy towards Daniel.

However, there are many who need to be rebuked from this point, as they resist God and do not come and yield immediately. Just like the others, a little thing will not affect them; much effort is required. So, whether it is a little or a lot, they are not presently moved.

Well, know that every time God speaks to you and your heart is not touched, you are missing an opportunity for eternal life. Yes, it is a significant opportunity, and your eternal life is lost every time God speaks to you and you do not yield to Him. Isn't that a great loss?

Secondly, know this: If you don't yield at first upon hearing the Word, it is less likely that you will yield later. If the corn doesn't sprout and rise within a certain time, it will never rise. Similarly, if the heart resists for too long, it may be too late for the Word to work on it.

Furthermore, understand this: if you persistently resist God, even if God doesn't eventually work on you, you will have much more trouble in your heart and conscience. Just like an old wound, the healing process is more troublesome. Therefore, I urge the Lord to work on your hearts immediately. And this is an exhortation from God: when you hear His Word, embrace it immediately and yield to it without delay. Whatever truth you hear, be convinced of it; whatever admonition you hear, embrace it right away.

First, what will be true in the future is true now. And each of you will wish in the future that you had yielded and submitted to the Word. If you will wish for it in the future, then there is a reason to do it now. Oh, how true the Word will be when you come to your sick bed and death bed. It is true now.

Secondly, as far as you know, whatever God speaks to your heart, He speaks to you as if it were the last time. The very first speaking may be the last, as far as you know. Sometimes it may be different, but you cannot make any promises, so yield to the Word immediately.

Thirdly, God may place you in a condition where if He doesn't grant mercy to your soul immediately, you are eternally lost. Sinners often find themselves in such a condition, where eternity hangs on the present moment. You may be put in a situation where either God must hear you immediately, or you are lost forever. Therefore, be willing to listen to God.

Lastly, consider the infinite patience of God thus far, as you have resisted for so long. Hasn't God spared your life? Oh, then you must be cautious about resisting any longer.

Yes, how often have you listened to temptations? They come to wickedness and you readily embrace them. So, when the Word comes close to your heart and speaks to your conscience, why can't you embrace it as well? Oh, when the Word comes near, especially so close that you can't deny that the Lord intended it for you this day, don't resist any longer, but yield and submit to Him immediately.

But Lord, I have resisted for a long time. What should I do?

It is a dreadful evil, and you should be willing to endure much because you have resisted for so long. Yes, but what if God were to speak one word to you now? What is your resolution? I ask this of the conscience of each person in this congregation: if God were to speak something today that specifically concerns you, are you resolved in your heart to fall down before Him, yield, and submit?

If you were to hear any threat in God's Word against your sin, are you now resolved, to the best of your ability, to renounce that sin? I ask you, will you do this, yes or no? What answer would you give to God if He were to speak today (since I have come by His providence) something from His Word that condemns my sin? I am resolved today, without further delay until sickness or death-bed, to do what I can, with God enabling me, to renounce those things that the Word of God condemns. Do you have such a resolution?

I would like to present some Scriptures, especially to those of you who are most ignorant, although some of you may already be familiar with them. Whether you know them or not, I will now present them in the name of God to those who have lived in these sins to this day and have not been humbled before God upon hearing the Word that I am about to speak to you.

Consider the Scripture in Romans 1:18. Pay attention to what God is saying to your soul now: "For the wrath of God is revealed from heaven against all ungodliness and unrighteousness of men, who by their unrighteousness suppress the truth." This is the Word of God to you today. Doesn't your conscience tell you that there are ways of ungodliness and unrighteousness in which you live? Now God from heaven tells you that His wrath is revealed against your soul if you do not repent. Oh, hear this word and let your soul be humbled and repent before God. And you, who hold the truth of God in unrighteousness, that is, you who have convicted consciences and yet go against them, you are the ones who suppress the truth in unrighteousness, and the wrath of God from heaven is revealed against you.

Now, let's specifically address the sin of swearing. Consider these two tests of Scripture and see if your hearts will yield to them. In Jeremiah 23:10, it is written: "For the land is full of adulterers; because of the curse the land mourns." We know that the land mourns today, and if you want to know the cause, you can attribute it to this fact: the Scripture says that because of swearing, the land mourns. Yes, because of your oaths, they are part of the cause of all the misery in the kingdom today. The Lord tells you this, and if your heart were tender, you would humble yourself before the Lord because of this and go away with a resolved heart against your sin.

And in that passage in Zechariah 5:3, it condemns not only the sin of stealing but also the sin of swearing. Then he said to me, "This is the curse that goes out over the face of the whole land. For everyone who steals shall be cleaned out according to what is on one side, and everyone who swears falsely shall be cleaned out according to what is on the other side." Here is a large flying scroll, twenty cubits in length and ten cubits in width, and this flying scroll represents the curse that goes out over the face of the whole land for everyone who steals and everyone who swears falsely. Oh, this word now has as much power to work on your heart as the word that affected Josiah. Are you resolved against these sins or not? This is what God declares to you today. Therefore, if your heart is tender, you will go home and humble your soul before God in your private place because of your sin.

And concerning the sin of Sabbath-breaking, in Ezekiel 20:13 (I want to test whether it may have an effect on some of your hearts today), it is written: "But the house of Israel rebelled against me in the wilderness. They did not walk in my statutes but rejected my rules, by which, if a person does them, he shall live; and my Sabbaths they greatly profaned." Then I said I would pour out my wrath upon them in the wilderness, to make an end of them. This is what God renews to you today. You are either resolved to continue in the practice of breaking God's Sabbaths or not. If you are resolved, this is the text that concerns you, and you should expect that it will be fulfilled upon you, that the Lord will pour out His wrath upon you to bring about your destruction. But when you hear this text, if your heart falls and yields, and you are humbled before the Lord, oh, that is good and right. The word has achieved its intended result. Surely, if Josiah had heard a word like this, his heart would have melted.

And now, concerning the sin of sexual immorality, I will share with you two passages from God's Word. They are dreadful ones, and I believe Josiah never heard such words read to him as I will read to you against this sin. The first is from Proverbs 22:14. "The mouth of forbidden women is a deep pit; he with whom the LORD is angry will fall into it." Here is a passage for all those wicked individuals who are enticed by the words of forbidden women. Take heed to what God is saying to your soul today. The person who is abhorred by God will fall into this pit. What a dreadful statement! Can anyone speak more dreadfully than this, that the one who is abhorred by God will fall into the pit of sexual immorality? And how many of you have fallen into that pit! Either you must acknowledge the Word of God or not. If not, you are atheists. And if this is not God's Word, then there is nothing in God's Word that you can rely on for your salvation. What do you rest upon for salvation if not on the Word? And if you rest upon any part of it, why not on this? Certainly, there is as much authority and power in this passage to humble as there is to save. And in the name of God, I do not merely read it but speak it to you from God's Word: the person who is abhorred by God will fall into the pit of sexual immorality. Now, you must decide whether to go away with a resolution to disregard or neglect the Word, or to continue in your sinful ways, or to be humbled before God because of the evil that God's Word so dreadfully speaks against. It would be a dreadful thing if anyone in this congregation were to leave with either a disregard for or a resolve to continue in their sinful ways. Oh, may the Lord accompany the reading of this passage to you as He did when the book was read to Josiah, so that the Lord may find a soul who will fall down and tremble before Him this day and give Him glory!

The other scripture is found in 2 Peter 2:9-10. "The Lord knows how to rescue the godly from trials, and to keep the unrighteous under punishment until the day of judgment, and especially those who indulge in the lust of defiling passion and despise authority." The Lord knows how to keep all wicked individuals for the day of judgment, but especially those who indulge in the desires of the flesh and engage in immoral actions. Now, some of you may dismiss this and say that you have not been flagrantly wicked in the actual sin of sexual immorality. But pay attention to the Word of the Lord in Romans 8:13. "For if you live according to the flesh, you will die." That is, you will perish eternally. If you find your comforts in gratifying the desires of the flesh, even if not in such wicked ways of sexual immorality, you will face eternal death.

However, despite all this, some may still leave guilty and hardened in their sin as they came. Therefore, I will read one more scripture to you, found in Deuteronomy 29:19-20. "One who, when he hears the words of this sworn covenant, blesses himself in his heart, saying, 'I shall be safe, though I walk in the stubbornness of my heart.' This will lead to the sweeping away of moist and dry alike. The LORD will not be willing to forgive him, but rather the anger of the LORD and his jealousy will smoke against that man, and the curses written in this book will settle upon him, and the LORD will blot out his name from under heaven." For those who still bless themselves in their wickedness and say, "Despite what the minister says, I will be at peace," oh, may the Lord impress this word upon you. I read it specifically because I fear that many in this place never read Scripture in their families. Therefore, I desire that they may encounter such scripture passages in this ordained gathering. Perhaps this very passage was one of the texts read to Josiah. Now you hear it read again. May the Lord bless these few sentences of scripture that are read to you from His Word, so that you may leave with tender hearts, humbled before the Lord, and resolved against your sin. But let us move on to the next point, which is that a tender heart is highly pleasing to God, for "because your heart was tender."

This is what I had planned to spend most of the time on: what the Scripture refers to as a tender heart. It is also called by other names elsewhere, such as a contrite heart, a broken heart, but especially what we find in Ezekiel as a heart of flesh. This is exactly the same thing. David is described as a man after God's own heart, and this is particularly because he had a very tender and easily moved heart. Now, in discussing this point, I will first try to explain what a tender heart is. This can be done in two ways: by describing its characteristics and by highlighting the difference between a tender heart and mere emotional sensitivity, temporary reactions to the Word, or the fear brought by the Law. However, this may be better addressed in the application.

For now, let us focus on understanding the true essence of a tender heart, and then we will explore its preciousness—how highly esteemed it is by God and how God reveals His remarkable acceptance of a tender heart.

According to the philosophers, a soft thing is one that easily yields to touch, while a hard thing resists touch with great effort. So, here is the first point: a tender heart is one that readily yields to God, it responds to God's touch. Just as wool easily gives way when you touch it, whereas a stone does not yield, or as flesh yields when touched but iron does not, a heart that yields to God is soft and tender. On the other hand, a heart that resists God is hard. When a person readily yields to the touch of God's Word, they are easily convinced by it and do not object to it. Their conscience easily acknowledges and applies the Word to themselves, and their will humbly submits to the Word. Even if their heart had previously pursued wickedness, when the Word confronts it, their will surrenders to God's Word. Such a soul says, "Let God's Word prevail, not my will." And the affections also surrender to the Word of God. This is a sign of a tender heart.

Yes, not only does a tender heart yield to God, but it also yields to others. The tenderness of heart is revealed in one's readiness to yield to others. If there is anything that justifiably offends their brothers and sisters, they willingly yield. They do not stubbornly hold on to anything to satisfy their own will, but if they recognize that it may legitimately offend others, they yield.

Secondly, a tender heart is characterized by sensitivity. It is a heart that is keenly aware and responsive. Just as the flesh feels it when pricked with a pin, a heart of flesh is sensitive to what is said to it. It is aware of God's displeasure. The thought of incurring God's displeasure deeply affects the heart, for it recognizes the weightiness of God's disapproval.

And it is aware of its own wretchedness and vileness, to the point of even despising itself before the Lord. It is sensitive to the Word, deeply responsive to it. Indeed, it is so sensitive to anything from God, any manifestation of His displeasure, and to its own sin or what the Word declares, that it becomes overwhelmed before God. There is no worldly comfort that can prevent it from faltering. A tender heart is not simply about being susceptible to a certain extent, but about being so acutely sensitive that it would undoubtedly faint under the weight of God's displeasure if God Himself did not come in to support and aid that soul. This is why in Deuteronomy 20:3, the word translated as "a fainting heart" is the same word used in my text, "let not your hearts be made tender or faint." This is the true tenderness, when there is such a tenderness of heart, such sensitivity to God's displeasure and one's own wretchedness, and to the Word, that it would faint before the Lord if the Lord did not uphold it by His Spirit.

Moreover, it is also sensitive to all of God's mercies, aware of its own unfaithfulness towards God, and appreciative of all the kindness it receives from Him. The kindness of God breaks this heart and melts it. It is like the sun shining upon ice, causing it to thaw. Similarly, the beams of God's mercy continually melt the heart of someone with such a tender disposition as we are discussing. A person who is less affected is less afflicted, indicating a hard heart. But a heart that is soft and tender is not only affected by its own sin and God's displeasure, but also by God's mercy. The heart melts in response to the apprehension of both mercy and sin.

Likewise, it is highly aware of the suffering of others. Why should our brethren be in a more difficult situation than we are? We are just as unworthy as they are. Tender hearts reason in this way, and their hearts even melt before God when they grasp the suffering of others. They find it astonishing that they, who are so undeserving, should enjoy peace, freedom, and comfort while their brethren endure such hardships. But hard-hearted individuals do not care; as long as they can be comfortable and have their needs met, they are indifferent. However, a tender heart is a sensitive heart. Furthermore, a tender heart is both yielding and discerning without causing a commotion. It does not make a fuss. This is true tenderness and the melting of the heart. You know that something tender yields, and flesh is sensitive. Metals melt and yield, and they do so silently; they make no noise. Similarly, a truly tender and melting heart is highly receptive to God and acutely aware of its own sin without making a clamour. Those men and women who are humbled by their sin and cause a disturbance in the family where they live, behaving in a violent manner, are not exhibiting genuine Gospel tenderness. This is not the true melting of the spirit. When you throw something into the fire, it creates a lot of noise as soon as it feels the heat. However, when metal feels the heat of the fire, it simply falls down and yields without making any noise. Likewise, when God makes a truly tender and melting heart sensitive to sin, it is so profoundly sensitive that it does not make a great noise but handles things quietly.

You might ask, "How can we remain calm when we perceive so much danger due to our sin?"

Yes, my brethren, this is the mystery of godliness in true Gospel humility. Keep this in mind, those of you who do not yet comprehend it, and remember it for those times when the Lord affects your hearts regarding your sin.

And then, fourthly, it is a heart that is receptive to any impression from God, or can be moulded into any shape that God desires. Just like melting a piece of wax allows you to create any desired impression on it, but trying to put a seal on a stone will not leave any mark. Only tender things can take an impression.

So, a tender heart is present before the Lord and is ready to receive any stamp that the Word of God puts upon it. Whatever holiness is in God's Word, according to its capacity, it leaves an imprint on the heart. After hearing the Word, the truths are clearly visible in the heart. Similarly, like soft objects that can be easily moulded, or molten metal that can be poured into any mould and take its shape, a tender heart can be moulded into whatever God desires, following the mould of His Word. We have a remarkable scripture for this in Romans 6:17 (I find it surprising how those words are translated in some versions of the New Testament). It should be translated as follows: "You have obeyed from the heart that form of doctrine into which you were delivered." So, you have obediently conformed your heart to the form of doctrine into which the Spirit of God delivered you. The form of doctrine is likened to a mould, and the human heart to molten metal. The Spirit of God, like a founder, takes the molten heart and pours it into the mould. Although the heart may have had a different form before, it now becomes shaped according to the mould. This is how it works with a tender and melting heart. A sinner who has lived in a certain sinful and wicked lifestyle for a long time encounters the Word of God, and the heat of God's Word begins to melt their heart. Then, the Spirit of God comes and takes the heart of this old sinner and puts it into the mould of the Word, transforming them into a vessel of honour.

Now, these five aspects can help us understand the nature of a tender heart, and you can use them to examine whether your hearts are tender or not. We could have discussed several other points to further elucidate the nature of a tender heart, but I prefer to leave them for the application.

# Chapter Six

# SERMON VI

## The Preciousness of a Tender Heart

"Because thine heart was tender" - 2 Kings 22:19

The Preciousness of a Tender Heart.

All I will do now is to demonstrate to you the preciousness of this tender heart and how God accepts it. Then I will conclude with words of comfort for those who possess such tender spirits.

Firstly, understand that it is very precious because it is a special fruit of the covenant of grace wherever it is found. Does your heart begin to soften towards God? Surely, this is a result of God's heart melting towards you first, through the means of the covenant of grace. Those heart-melting provisions within the covenant of grace begin to flow into your life when your heart starts to melt towards God. In Ezekiel 36, it is a clear text, interpreted by all divines as a promise of the covenant of grace and a special fruit of it. In verse 26, there is a promise: "A new heart also will I give you, and a new spirit I will put within you, and I will take away the stony heart out of your flesh, and I will give you a heart of flesh. And I will put my spirit within you, and cause you to walk in my statutes, and ye shall keep my judgments and do them." A new heart! Every person naturally has a hard heart. Although some people's hearts may appear softer than others, everyone in the world has a hard heart. So, what is this new heart that God promises to give? It is the removal of the stony heart and the gift of a heart of flesh. Here lies the fruit of the covenant of grace. Whoever possesses this tender heart is undoubtedly received into the covenant of grace, which demonstrates its immense preciousness. For all things associated with the covenant of grace are precious, as the covenant itself is precious. The treasures of God's grace in the covenant are truly precious, and a tender heart is one of the choice jewels found within those treasures. When God gives you a tender heart, He is giving you this valuable jewel from the treasures of the covenant of grace.

Certainly, even if God were to grant you kingdoms to possess, or the entire world, it would be nothing compared to this gift. For God can give the possession of this world to someone whom He will never enter into a covenant with; God can bestow all this world out of His general bounty and patience. I remember Luther saying about the entire empire of the Turk, "It is only a crumb that the great householder, the Lord, throws to his dog." But this tenderness of heart is a fruit of the covenant of grace, and to have even the smallest fruit of the covenant of grace is a greater mercy than having all the fruits of God's general bounty and patience.

Secondly, a tender heart is very precious because it contains many graces as its ingredients. Indeed, the heart of a person becomes supple and tender through the composition and mixture of many of God's Spirit's graces. The oil that softens the heart of a sinner is a blend of numerous graces. In fact, all the graces of God's Spirit are the ingredients in this composition that softens the heart of a sinner. You can see humility, faith, wisdom, patience, and any other grace you can think of in this composition. God sees all the graces.

I remember Chrysostom expressing what I am now preaching about, the tenderness of spirit and its excellence. He said, "When the Spirit of God works this tenderness, it is like a lady who is creating a precious compound, a sovereign balm. She has all her noble maidens attending to her, and she calls one to fetch one ingredient and another to fetch another. She takes them all together and creates a sovereign balm, oil, or whatever she desires to make." Similarly, says Chrysostom, the Spirit of God gathers all graces to come and create this compound, this oil, to soften the heart of a sinner. The truth is, even though you, poor tender spirit, may not be able to see the distinct workings of those graces, they are present within you. It is like a prescribed oil or conserve from a physician made of specific ingredients. The physician tells you to take this mixture if you want to be cured. So you go to the apothecary with the prescription, and the apothecary gives you a small amount of oil or conserve in a glass. You may say, "But the physician told me there should be many ingredients." The apothecary replies, "Here it is, made from those ingredients, even if you can't discern them."

Likewise, in a soul, the scripture requires various graces such as faith, humility, patience, heavenly-mindedness, and others. Now, a poor sinner who has this tenderness of spirit often worries because they cannot find the exercise of specific graces. But if you have a tender spirit, you possess them all. They are all present within you, just like the oil that softened your heart. If any saving grace of God's Spirit had been lacking, your heart would never have reached this tenderness. This demonstrates the preciousness of a tender spirit.

Thirdly, another aspect that demonstrates the preciousness of a tender spirit is that it puts the soul in a state of readiness to receive mercy. It prepares the soul to receive any mercy that the Lord has to bestow. As Bernard said, "God does not pour the oil of His mercy except into a contrite heart," and this is certain. But when the heart is contrite and tender, the Lord immediately pours the oil of His mercy upon such a person. It is in a state of readiness to receive any mercy, and the Lord, who takes pleasure in mercy, surely will not miss the opportunity to display His glory when He sees a soul capable and prepared for it. Now your soul is made ready to receive any mercy that the Lord has to offer, and the Lord is infinitely willing to bestow mercy. The reason why anyone in the world lacks mercy is not because there is a shortage of it, but rather because their vessel is not ready to receive it. You may argue that God could make them ready, but God is not inclined to exert His almighty power to prepare every vessel. However, once it becomes evident that God has such love for a soul as to prepare a vessel for mercy, that soul can confidently conclude that there is more than enough mercy available. Perhaps you do not possess it at present, but one thing is certain: there is as much mercy for you as you can contain. I can say to you, just as the Lord says to His people in another context, "I know the thoughts that I have toward them, thoughts of peace and love." So, regardless of your fears and doubts, the Lord says to you, "I know the thoughts that I have toward this sinner, thoughts of love and mercy." I could provide you with many Scriptures to demonstrate how this disposition prepares the soul to receive mercy. One remarkable passage is found in Zechariah 12:10: "I will pour out on the house of David and the inhabitants of Jerusalem a spirit of grace and supplication. They will look on me, the one they have pierced, and they will mourn for him as one mourns for an only child." God promises to pour out His Spirit, and He describes the manner in which they will mourn.

Then, at the beginning of chapter 13, it says, "In that day there shall be a fountain opened, a fountain of mercy opened, and it shall flow into their hearts when they have such a spirit poured out upon them." Here, the spirit of grace and mourning are mentioned together. A tender heart is called a spirit of grace, not only because of God's free grace in it, but also because of the many graces of God that are poured into the heart when this spirit is poured into it. That's the third aspect.

Fourthly, another way in which the preciousness of this tender spirit is evident is that it makes the soul suitable for engaging in all the ordinances and ways of God. For example, it prepares the soul for hearing the word, just as Josiah did when he sanctified the name of God by listening to His word. And when it comes to receiving the sacrament, nothing is more fitting than this tenderness of spirit. Why? Because in the sacrament, we come to have communion with Jesus Christ, and as the text says, "From his fullness we have all received, grace upon grace." That means, just as the impression of a seal is left on wax, there is an impression for every impression. Whatever grace is in Christ, the same grace is imprinted upon the heart. Now, when we come to receive the sacrament, we come to have communion with Jesus Christ so that we may partake of His abundance. Furthermore, we come to have the seal of the covenant of grace placed upon our hearts, for that is the nature of a sacrament—it is the seal of the righteousness of faith. And what disposition of heart could be more suitable for a seal than a tender heart? When you come to the sacrament, it is crucial to bring soft hearts, to bring this tender heart with you, for you are bringing your hearts to have the seal of the covenant of grace placed upon them. Oh, this is a precious disposition that the Lord loves dearly. When a group of people comes to receive the sacrament, having softened their hearts beforehand and thus prepared their souls to receive the seal, it is highly regarded by the Lord. All of God's ways have a positive impact on a tender heart. Even the slightest mercy or beam of God's love can melt a tender heart, and that is why it is extremely precious in the eyes of God.

Fifthly, it brings great honour to God and exalts His name. There is no disposition in the world that honours the name of God more than a tender heart. It shows reverence for God, fears Him, acknowledges His sovereignty and power, and gives Him glory for His justice and mercy. This disposition glorifies God, just as a trembling heart, as I mentioned earlier, brings glory to God. A tender heart greatly magnifies the name of God.

Sixthly, it is a disposition that commends all our services to God and makes them acceptable. Without a tender heart, no service we perform can be pleasing to God in any way. I'm sure you're familiar with the well-known passage in Psalm 51. The prophet speaks of a contrite spirit, saying, "The sacrifices of God are a broken spirit; a broken and contrite heart, O God, you will not despise." Note that this broken and contrite heart is the same as the tender heart mentioned in the text. It is the sacrifice that pleases God, and sacrifices are mentioned in the plural form. This emphasizes the supreme value of a tender heart—it is the choice among all sacrifices. It is what God requires above all sacrifices.

Moreover, a tender heart is equivalent to all sacrifices. Even if you cannot offer anything else to God, if you can offer Him a tender spirit and a contrite heart, He will be well pleased. Many poor sinners complain and are troubled because they feel they can do very little for God. But if you can offer a tender spirit and a contrite heart to God, I assure you, it is equivalent to all sacrifices before Him.

And thirdly, the sacrifices that please God are a broken spirit. This means that a disposition of a broken and contrite heart commends any other sacrifice.

If this sacrifice is present, it is as if all other sacrifices were there, and anything offered with this disposition is acceptable, while nothing is acceptable without it. In Isaiah 66, the Lord says, "But this is the one to whom I will look: he who is humble and contrite in spirit and trembles at my word." It follows that anyone offering a sacrifice without a contrite and humble spirit is like someone who slays a man or cuts off a dog's neck—such sacrifices are rejected. What an excellent disposition it is that commends all our sacrifices and replaces all other sacrifices before the Lord.

Seventhly, furthermore, a tender heart is precious because it keeps one close to God and causes them to cleave to Him. It is a disposition that continuously keeps the heart near to God. If there is even a slight drifting in the soul of one who possesses a tender heart, they quickly perceive it and cannot rest until they return to God. If the Lord withdraws even a little, someone with a tender heart is aware of it. Thus, it is a precious disposition because it keeps the heart of a sinner close to God.

Lastly, a tender heart is a disposition that makes a person a valuable member in the church and society. It makes them a beneficial companion. Someone with a tender spirit is always harmless. A sour spirit is troublesome to live with, but a tender spirit yields to anything when shown the reason by God. They have a peaceful and gentle nature. Such an individual is highly aware of the well-being or harm of the community. Often, someone with a tender spirit is as sensitive to the good of others as they are to their own good. If you present anything that concerns the glory of God or the public good, they immediately become aware of it because of their tender spirit. On the other hand, if you propose something that does not concern their personal desires and satisfaction, others may not be sensitive to it. However, a tender spirit is receptive to anything you propose for God or the good of others. This is the excellence of a tender spirit. The Lord highly esteems and values this tender spirit.

First, there is the primary object that captures God's attention in the entire world. The Lord looks towards this person, as stated in Isaiah 66. God says, "But this is the one to whom I will look..." There is no object on the face of the Earth that draws God's eye more than this.

Secondly, God's heart is greatly inclined towards such an individual. Regarding Ephraim, we have a passage in Jeremiah 31:18. It says, "I have surely heard Ephraim bemoaning himself..." Ephraim sat alone, lamenting his condition and his heart began to break. Notice how God's heart is moved towards him in the twentieth verse. God asks, "Is Ephraim my dear son? Is he a pleasant child?" Despite speaking against him, God remembers Ephraim earnestly and His bowels are troubled for him. God declares, "I will surely have mercy upon him," says the Lord. If there is a soul that isolates itself, lamenting its own sin out of a genuine sense of its evil and the dishonour it has brought to God, the Lord looks upon such an individual with His heart inclined towards them. His compassion stirs within Him.

Thirdly, it is crucial to consider this principal aspect, which, if we were to say nothing more, would be sufficient. Jesus Christ is anointed by God the Father with a special purpose to be the comforter of such a heart. Wherever there is such a tender, broken, contrite heart (for these are different expressions of the same disposition), let that person know that God the Father has anointed His Son specifically to be the comforter of such a soul. This is clearly evident in Isaiah 61. It states, "The Spirit of the Lord God is upon me, because the Lord has anointed me to bring good news to the afflicted; he has sent me to bind up the broken-hearted..." and further on, "to grant to those who mourn in Zion—to give them a beautiful headdress instead of ashes, the oil of gladness instead of mourning, the garment of praise instead of a faint spirit..." The Spirit of the Lord God is upon Jesus Christ and He is anointed to preach good news to those with broken spirits, to console those who mourn, and to exchange their sorrow for joy. Surely, a soul cannot lack comfort when Jesus Christ is designated by God the Father in His role to provide comfort. He is a Christ for it, that He may bring comfort. When it is stated, "The Spirit of the Lord God is upon me, because the Lord has anointed me," it is essentially saying that the Lord God the Father has made me Christ, for the word "Christ" simply means "anointed." God has made me Christ so that I may preach good news to sinners with broken hearts. Here, God is accepting a tender spirit when He sends His Son out of His bosom and instructs Him to go into the world, making it a vital part of His mission to be a comforter to such tender spirits. He pours the oil of joy, which replaces the previous oil that softened their hearts and made them tender. And that concludes the third aspect.

Fourthly, there are numerous precious promises in Scripture, especially directed towards them (each one worth a kingdom). The Scripture refers to these promises as exceeding great and precious promises, and the saints consider their wealth to lie in these promises. One promise in Psalm 34, for instance, a person with a tender spirit would not trade it for the world: "The Lord is near to the brokenhearted and saves the crushed in spirit." And then there is another promise in Isaiah 57:15, which is even more comprehensive: "For thus says the One who is high and lifted up, who inhabits eternity, whose name is Holy: 'I dwell in the high and holy place, and also with him who is of a contrite and lowly spirit, to revive the spirit of the lowly, and to revive the heart of the contrite.'" My brethren, although heaven is a glorious dwelling place of God, it is not enough for Him. God does not consider it sufficient unless He also dwells in a tender, broken, humble spirit. That is the dwelling place that the Lord values, just as much as His dwelling in heaven. You know how great princes have various palaces in different countries. Similarly, the great King of the world keeps His court in heaven and in a contrite heart—those are the two principal places. Although the Lord encompasses the whole world and fills heaven and earth, His court is held in the highest heavens and the humblest heart. Take note, He is said to dwell with them. When a person passes by, they may be generous in passing, but their primary usefulness is found in their place of residence. While travelling, one can do good to some, but their greatest usefulness is in their dwelling. Likewise, although the Lord may bestow common favours as He passes by others, it is in the heart where He fully extends His mercy. God dwells in the heart; He resides there in a constant manner to communicate Himself to them. And for what purpose? He dwells with the contrite spirit to revive them. The living God is always dwelling with them. Even if your dwelling place is humble, even if it is a poor and dark abode where you must hide your head, having a contrite heart means that there is a glorious palace for the great King of heaven and earth to dwell in. We have many promises, such as "Blessed are those who mourn" and "Blessed are the poor in spirit," and so on. If we were to search the scriptures and consider what the Lord says about this disposition of a tender spirit, time would quickly pass. It is another way in which God manifests His high regard for them.

Fifthly, the Lord shows exceptional tenderness towards someone with a tender heart in times of affliction. If there is any burden upon a person with a tender spirit, the Lord knows that they are sensitive to it, and therefore He is aware of their condition. The Lord is just as aware of your condition as you are of your burden, and His utmost concern is that such a person never falters before Him. This is evident in Isaiah 57, where He says that He dwells with the humble and contrite spirit. He declares, "I will not contend forever, nor will I be angry always, for the spirit would grow faint before me, and the souls that I have made." God says, "I will not allow burdens to be constantly upon them, even though I may, for a specific purpose and for their good, manifest some displeasure for the time being. But I will not remain angry forever. I know they are sensitive to even the slightest displeasure from me, and therefore I will be tender towards them, those who have such tender hearts, so that their spirits do not grow faint before me when I come against them in anger." In Isaiah 27, the Lord affirms, "My anger is not in me, but if anyone sets briers and thorns before me, I will march against them and burn them up together. However, as for my own people, I will be tender towards them and show no fury." The Lord is tender towards those who have such tender spirits.

Sixthly, once again, He seals such individuals for mercy in times of public calamity. In Ezekiel 9, you can find that those who mourned for the committed sins were commanded by the Lord to be marked with the seal of preservation before the city was destroyed. Therefore, wherever there is a tender spirit, the Lord sets a seal of mercy upon them. Consequently, no matter what calamity befalls the place where such a person resides, they shall be marked for mercy. This was evident in the case of Josiah, as it was a special demonstration of the Lord's mercy towards him that he would not witness the impending calamity but be delivered before its arrival.

Furthermore, this leads to another manifestation of God's love towards a tender spirit. If the Lord foresees that calamities are imminent upon kingdoms, and He observes that the heart of a particular individual, whether male or female, is so tender that they would not be able to bear those calamities, the Lord, in His great love, takes them away to Himself before the calamities strike. This is best exemplified by the case of Josiah.

I must say, when the Lord sees men and women with tender spirits who are unable to bear witness to the grievous calamities that God intends for certain places, where He will manifest His severe displeasure, out of His great love, God takes them away beforehand. Just as Josiah was taken away, but not by the war of his own country or kingdom; the war against the kingdom did not occur until after God took Josiah away. Therefore, I have no doubt that the Lord has shown mercy to many of our forefathers who, in their time, lamented the sins of the kingdom. Some the Lord removed from our midst, while others He took away through death, for they were men and women of tender spirits. The Lord saw that they could not bear to witness and hear the dreadful things that we are reserved to witness and hear.

However, the truth is that the Lord has also reserved this hard-hearted generation. While we can hear of dreadful things happening, we are not truly sensitive to the suffering of others because it is at a distance from us. It seems that the Lord has reserved this generation to witness, hear, and experience dreadful things. He has taken away the tender-hearted generation. Just as a father would remove young and tender children from the sight of their mother having her breast cut off due to cancer or a similar disease, in order to spare them from witnessing her pain, God the Father takes away His tender-hearted servants when the Church, their spiritual mother, is about to endure severe afflictions. He does so because they are not able to bear the sight and hearing of such dreadful things. In doing this, God shows great respect for His servants. Many of His servants who have spent much time in solitary lamentation over the sins of the nation are now taken away from the impending evil, and the Lord has taken them up to Himself. If their hearts were so deeply affected, how would they be able to bear witnessing and hearing the things that we see and hear on this very day?

Application.

Now I will try to conclude with a few words of application. I had intended to explain how God reveals Himself to those with tender hearts and how they have the greatest influence in prayer. The Lord hears the prayers of the poor, He prepares their hearts, and inclines His ear to listen to their pleas.

Therefore, it is a very dangerous thing for anyone to harm someone with a tender heart. Let people be cautious, for God will ensure justice. God holds a mighty high regard for such individuals, and perhaps it is because they have tender and humble spirits. You might think you can take advantage of them, as they may not retaliate blow for blow. However, they withdraw and pour out their grievances to their Father, telling Him about all the wrongs you have done to them. In this way, they open their hearts to God and find solace. Many of you, when wronged by others, have no other way to find relief than to respond with anger and retaliation. But someone with a tender spirit has a better way to find comfort. They can retreat in solitude, allowing their hearts to soften before the Lord, and there they find solace.

Now, it is likely to go very poorly for you if you have wronged such individuals. It would be better for you to wrong a hundred other people than to wrong them. Imagine if you have a child who has a gentle and tender spirit, someone who does not immediately resort to fighting. And then someone wrongs that child, and with tears in their eyes, they come to you to express their grievance. Wouldn't it stir up your spirit to protect and defend your child, especially because you know your child has a gentle and tender disposition? Certainly, it is the same with God. God will ensure justice for them. I recall hearing about a prominent woman in Scotland who professed that she was more afraid of the fasting and prayer of John Knox and his followers than of an army of one hundred thousand men. So, always be cautious about causing harm to men and women with tender spirits, for God holds them in high esteem.

And for those of you who have tender spirits, I hope you take what has been said as your portion and rejoice in it. Perhaps God has not given you much of this world's possessions, but He has given you a tender heart, and that is infinitely more valuable. Maybe you have weak memories and abilities, and you cannot do what others can. However, hasn't God given you a tender and compassionate heart? That is worth more than all the riches in the world.

Let it comfort you in light of the weakness of your virtues. Yes, your virtues may be weak, but they are compensated by this tenderness. It is a profound question whether God values someone who excels in all virtues but lacks brokenness of heart, or someone who excels in brokenness of heart despite weaknesses in other virtues. Although brokenness of heart encompasses other virtues, it can still be prominent even when other virtues are weak. This is because, in addition to the mixture of other virtues, there is the presence of the Spirit of God. The Spirit of God can activate and animate a particular grace in the soul, allowing someone who is weak in other areas to excel in brokenness of heart. Thus, even if you are weak in other virtues, you possess an excellence that is as remarkable as those who have greater virtues.

Perhaps you have a temperament that prevents you from listening attentively or obeying the word as you desire. However, can you feel? Do you have tenderness of spirit? Certainly, where there is a sense of feeling, there is life. So as long as you have that sensitivity, there is life within you.

Likewise, let it bring comfort to you in the face of all your fears. You fear God's wrath, but if you have a tender heart, the Lord will ensure that you never experience great displeasure. Because you have already sanctified the name of God, and you are sensitive to even the slightest display of His displeasure, it is certain that you will never encounter overwhelming displeasure from God.

And find comfort in this: Jesus Christ's sorrows are for you; you have a share in the sorrows of Jesus Christ. Although you have a mournful spirit, remember that you should not solely rely on the tenderness of your own heart, but rather look up to Christ who had a tender spirit.

If the tenderness in your heart is genuine, it is like the oil that flowed from Aaron's head down to his garments, from Christ your head down to His members. Christ Himself was one who had a very tender spirit. The tenderness that was in Christ now belongs to you. He was tender during His time on Earth, and He remains tender now and will have a tender heart even on the day of judgment. This is something that your soul should rejoice in and find comfort.

But you may wonder, "Lord, how can I be sure that these comforts truly belong to me? Can I apply them too soon and be presumptuous?"

I will give you one key to help you know with certainty whether these comforts belong to you or not.

Does hearing these things and applying them to your hearts make your hearts more tender? Do they soften your hearts further towards God? If you find that upon hearing this, your hearts become more tender instead of hardened, and if you feel humbled, loathing yourselves and abhorring your own sins before the Lord even more when you hear that He accepts you, then it truly belongs to you, it is your portion, and you can safely embrace it. Let me provide you with a Scripture to safely bring this comfort into your souls: In Ezekiel 36, where the Lord promised a tender heart in verse 26, God also promised to remove the heart of stone and give a heart of flesh. Now pay attention to one particular result of having a heart of flesh. After making various gracious promises of saving them from uncleanness and bestowing numerous mercies, the text says in verse 31, "Then you will remember your evil ways and your deeds that were not good, and you will loathe yourselves for your iniquities and abominations." Can this be applied to today? Can you say, "I heard a sermon about a tender heart, how precious it is and how God accepts it, and at that moment, my heart broke. I remembered my unworthy ways before God. Oh, how I walked so undeserving of His mercies and so wretchedly in His sight!" If you can say this, if at that time and during that sermon it was so, then peace be with you, for it is all your portion, and may it bring you much good. Embrace it, cherish your tenderness of spirit, and hold onto it if you want to maintain your comfort.

# Chapter Seven

# SERMON VII

## Because thine heart was tender

"Because thine heart was tender" - 2 Kings 22:19

Let's move on from what was previously discussed and continue.

Objection: But someone may say, "This is the great thing that I find lacking in me, the absence of a tender spirit. If I could find my heart tender, then I could truly be comforted, despite the many hardships. Oh, the hardness and insensibility of my heart."

Answer: To that, I respond as follows: First, if you are aware of your hardness, then there is certainly some degree of tenderness present. We cannot be aware of hardness without tenderness. Do you consider the lack of tenderness to be one of the greatest evils that can befall you? Many complain about difficult times, saying, "We have hard times." But a poor soul may say, "Oh, I have a hard heart, and the hardness within my heart is a greater evil than all the hardships of the times." Surely, it is an indication that there is tenderness in the heart when one is so aware of its hardness. For you know that when the flesh is affected by a disease and becomes tough and hard, it is not sensitive at all, not even to its own hardness. However, once you become aware of the hardness, God has begun to work tenderness in you.

Secondly, there are two kinds of hardness: the hardness of a stone and the hardness of ice. God says He will take away the heart of stone. You know that a stone, no matter how intensely the sun's rays shine upon it, never yields. But ice, though it is very hard, melts and thaws when the warm beams of the sun shine upon it. So even if you feel your heart is hard at present, when the beams of God's love shine upon your heart, when the rays of God's grace manifested in the Gospel illuminate your soul, how do you find your heart responding then? Oh, then my heart begins to yield. Then my heart surrenders to God. That is a sign that it is not the hardness of a stone. If the beams of God's love and the grace of God in the Gospel can melt your heart, if you find in your heart that if God were to reveal His grace to you in His Son and pour out His love in your heart, you believe your heart would yield and melt before Him. I say, that is not the hardness of a stone. The hardness of heart that is so contrary to the Covenant of Grace. It is possible for one's heart to be occasionally hard in the present, but even then, it will melt under the warm beams of the sun. However, the heart of stone is what is truly contrary to the Covenant of Grace.

Answer 3: You feel in your heart that you cannot mourn for your sin, for that is what you mean when you say your heart is so hard. But let me pose this to you: At the time when you cannot mourn as you desire, is your heart not averse to sin? Is it not set against sin? Would you not choose, if given the choice, to endure all the miseries in the world rather than willfully commit any sin against God? And this choice does not arise merely from a sense of necessity, but from a disposition in your heart that is opposed to sin. You have such opposition to sin that you would turn away from it rather than from all other evils and afflictions in the world. Now, peace be to you if this is true. Even when you think your heart is so hard that you cannot mourn for sin, there is still comfort for you. And there are two reasons for this.

Firstly, it is an indication of great love for God that even though the Lord may not make you as deeply aware, in terms of your emotions, of the bitterness and evil of sin, your heart is strongly opposed to it. It is not as much a sign of grace when the Lord fills the heart with anguish, sorrow, and bitterness for sin, and then the heart turns away from it. But when the heart turns away from the evil of sin more than from any other affliction, even at a time when it does not feel the full extent of the bitterness of sin or the displeasure of God towards sin, this indeed indicates much grace.

Again, this is a comfort in the second place because you have that which God specifically aims for in making people's hearts sensitive to sin and causing them to mourn for it. What does God desire in the mourning of men and women? It is that they may turn away from their sin and value His mercy. God does not take pleasure in causing grief to His children. He cares for your mourning only to the extent that it may turn your hearts away from sin and cause you to value His grace. Now, if you are so aware of the evil of your sin that it turns your heart away from it and makes you value God's grace, then surely you possess the tenderness of heart that the Scripture calls for. This is what God accepts.

Let me illustrate this with an example. Imagine there are two sick men. One cries out in intense pain, experiencing extreme agony, and screams and shrieks in the midst of his suffering. He sends for a physician, desperately seeking relief. On the other hand, there is another man who is also sick, but he is not in as much pain. He does not cry out as loudly as the first man. However, he understands the seriousness and danger of his sickness to the extent that he is willing to do everything he can to call for the physician's help. He is even willing to give up all his possessions in order to receive assistance. Although he may not cry out as much as the first man, if he is sensible enough to take any action and values his healing more than his possessions, this man may be healed just as quickly as the other. The physician may come to help him just as soon. Similarly, some individuals become so deeply aware of the evil of their sin that they are overwhelmed by its weight. They may cry out and lament in a dreadful manner. All they can do is pursue Christ and seek Him above all else for help. They are willing to give up everything for Christ. On the other hand, there are those who may not experience such extreme sorrow, but they still apprehend Christ and value Him above all else. I say, if you fall into the latter category, although not in the same intensity of sorrow, you possess the tenderness of heart that God works in the Covenant of Grace for those whom He loves and intends to save eternally. Therefore, comfort yourself with what you have heard about the excellence of a tender spirit. Since it is so precious, strive to maintain it. This leads to the third point: if God has granted you any tenderness of spirit, it is a jewel worth more than if He had made you an emperor or a queen, as you heard the previous day. Therefore, keep it within your heart. Work diligently to maintain your tenderness, for know that although the Lord works tenderness in our hearts, without carefulness, there is a great danger of becoming hardened once again. Have you not experienced this? Have you not felt your hearts yielding and melting before God for a time, only to find them hardened again shortly after? Certainly, if you are familiar with your own heart, you will recognize this. Therefore, while you feel God working tenderness, strive to maintain it. Pray to the Lord to preserve it in your heart. "O Lord, keep this in the thoughts and purposes of my heart forever."

Question: You may ask, how should we maintain tenderness in our spirit?

Answer: First of all, search deeply into the riches of God's grace in the Covenant. Make an effort to understand the glorious abundance of grace in the Covenant of Grace. There is nothing that works more effectively to cultivate and preserve tenderness than the wonderful mercy of God in Jesus Christ. Those heart-blood mercies of God in Christ, those tender expressions of God's mercies and compassions in Christ, are what both create and maintain tenderness of heart. The more a person meditates on these mercies, delving into their depths, the more tenderness they will acquire and preserve in their hearts.

Secondly, be extremely cautious about falling into any known sin. Nothing hardens the heart more than indulging in known or gross sins. The daily struggles with sin in the lives of the saints do not harden them, but if they fall into a significant sin, it often leads to a great hardening of their hearts for an extended period of time. Reestablishing tenderness becomes a challenging task. This was the case with David when he committed a grave sin. His heart was hardened for almost an entire year. For three-quarters of a year, his heart remained hardened. He had lost the tenderness he had before. Although he initially said he would confess his sin, he did not truly confess it until Nathan confronted him. This delay in sincere confession lasted for three-quarters of a year. During that time, he remained in his sin, and his heart was greatly hardened, losing the fear of God in his soul. Therefore, be cautious and avoid falling into gross sins.

We can draw a parallel from the story of manna. Although the beams of the sun would melt manna, the fire would bake and harden it. Similarly, the heart of a Christian is like manna in this regard. The beams of God's grace in Christ and the mercies of the Covenant melt the heart, so you should keep your heart under the influence of those beams. However, the fire of any sinful desire bakes and hardens the heart. Therefore, be cautious and avoid falling into gross sins.

And indeed, that one argument should be sufficient, one would think, to prevent a gracious heart from yielding to the strength of temptation. When a temptation arises to commit a particular sin, which may strongly appeal to your fleshly desires, some may have certain arguments against it while others may have different ones. Perhaps you are struck with fear and horror, and your conscience would condemn you if you were to commit it. But a gracious heart should have this prevailing thought: if I give in to this sin, I will lose my tenderness, my heart will be hardened as a result. Someone who knows the sweetness of tenderness should be unwilling to lose it for the sake of gaining the whole world. Regardless of what may happen to me, let me hold on to my tenderness, says a gracious heart.

Not only gross sins that a Christian may fall into, but also formality in performing duties will harden your heart. If you grow accustomed to a formal approach in your duties, you will lose the tenderness of your heart. It is essential for you to maintain communion with God in your holy duties. Do not be satisfied with merely going through the motions of duty unless you experience the sunshine of God's presence in those duties. On the other hand, ensure that your heart is engaged and turned towards God in the performance of those duties. When men and women carry out their duties merely out of a sense of obligation, driven by a slave-like conscience, they may continue to perform them, but their hearts will grow harder and harder over time, eventually abandoning the duties altogether. Those who rely solely on the compulsion of conscience to fulfill their duties will eventually give them up. However, when a heart realizes that it used to enjoy communion with God in the performance of duties, and that those duties were occasions of sweet interaction with God, they will continue to perform them. They cannot be satisfied with the performance of any duty unless they feel God's presence entering their souls. This is truly a soul that will maintain tenderness of heart. When grace is kept in exercise, the heart will remain tender.

Fourthly, another rule for maintaining the tenderness of your heart is this: be cautious of the company you keep. Beware of associating with those who have hard and frivolous spirits, especially among those who profess religion but lack seriousness. Being in the company of such individuals greatly hardens the heart. On the other hand, keeping the company of those who have broken spirits and tender hearts before the Lord has a significant effect in preserving the tenderness of your own heart. Often, when your heart starts to harden, encountering a soft-hearted and broken-hearted Christian, whose heart melts before the Lord, can cause your own heart to melt as well. Therefore, seek the company of broken and tender-hearted Christians. In the interactions with fellow believers, there is great power in maintaining tenderness of spirit. This is why the Apostle exhorts in Hebrews 3:12, "Take heed, brethren, lest there be in any of you an evil heart of unbelief, in departing from the living God. But exhort one another daily, while it is called 'today,' lest any of you be hardened through the deceitfulness of sin." Exhort one another. This means coming together and engaging in conversations with spiritual Christians who are lively, active, and stirring. Encourage one another. Why? So that none of you may be hardened by the deceitfulness of sin. When Christians gather and discuss the goodness of God in Christ, the profound mysteries of the Gospel, and the work of God in their hearts, with each one sharing their experiences and encounters with God, it serves as a remarkable aid in keeping the heart in a state of gracious tenderness.

There are other means that could be mentioned, such as...

Fifthly, be cautious of being too focused on earthly and worldly matters. If you let your heart excessively pursue lawful things, it will harden your heart. Even though those things may be lawful in themselves, if you give your heart inordinate attachment to them, you will eventually become earthly, dull, and insensitive. Just as earth quickly hardens into stone, when your heart becomes attached to worldly things, even if they are lawful, you will rapidly lose the tenderness of your heart. A worldly Christian can never be a tender-hearted Christian. However, this shall be sufficient for this point.

Now, since a tender heart is highly valued by the Lord, we have reason to lament, and lament deeply, the lack of it. This applies not only to people in general but also to Christians. Oh, how little tenderness of spirit can the Lord find even among His own people! Our hearts have become hardened. God's name is fearfully dishonoured, His law is wickedly violated, His wrath is dreadfully revealed, His severe displeasure is threatened, His judgments are inflicted, and we have reason to fear ruin and destruction. Yet, people's hearts remain hardened. Even though God's compassionate nature is moved, and His heart-blood mercies are extended, and His gracious promises are revealed, and His heart-melting promises and overwhelming goodness are manifested, and His grace is abundantly poured out in the world, still, the hearts of people remain hardened. The hearts of people are generally like the creature described in Job 41, around verse 24. The text says, "His heart is as firm as a stone, yes, as hard as a piece of the nether millstone."

Truly, the hearts of most men and women are like the heart of the creature mentioned earlier, resembling a blacksmith's anvil. No matter how many times we strike them, they do not soften but rather harden. They are like the blacksmith's dog that lies beneath the anvil, unaffected by the sparks flying around its ears, able to sleep soundly. Similarly, many people, even when God's wrath is dreadfully revealed from heaven and sparks fly around them, have hardened hearts that cannot repent (Romans 2:5). Woe, woe to us who have sinned against the Lord, but even greater woe to us whose hearts have hardened in our sin. Where is the spirit of Elijah, the spirit of David, the spirit of Hezekiah, the spirit of Josiah? Where is the spirit of Jeremiah and Daniel and other tender-hearted individuals mentioned in Scripture? It seems as though that spirit has departed from the world.

The hearts of people are not only hard like iron, but they are like stones. There is a difference between the hardness of iron and that of stone. Iron, though hard, can yield when put into fire and be melted by intense heat. But when you put a stone into fire, it will never yield; instead, it may burst and fly in your face. Many people are not only as hard as iron, but they are as stone. Even when they are in the fire, they do not yield but rather complain about God, His ways, and His severity, instead of acknowledging the wickedness of their own hearts. You can see that the hearts of people are not only like iron but like stone, or even worse than stone. We read that the stones split apart at the resurrection of Jesus Christ. Bonaventure, though a Catholic, reflects on this and exclaims, "Lord, You have said that You will take away the heart of stone and give a heart of flesh. But Lord, give me a heart of stone, that I may be made aware of the glorious things of Christ. For I read that the stones split apart as if they were aware of the death and resurrection of Jesus Christ, but I cannot feel anything when I hear and read about the death and resurrection of Jesus Christ. Therefore, Lord, give me a heart of stone." There is a great deal of hardness in the hearts of people, and it is a grave and significant evil. Luther has an expression: "Just as the contrite heart is a sacrifice that is so acceptable to God, the hard heart is a sacrifice that is so acceptable to the devil." And to demonstrate a little the evil of a hard heart and some convictions regarding it, let me elaborate on the evil of hardness of heart.

Firstly, if you have a hard heart, you are a wicked person (Proverbs 21:29). A wicked person hardens their face, and this expression signifies the hardness within their heart, which is contrary to uprightness.

Moreover, know that it is one of the most terrifying judgments that can be inflicted upon a sinner in this world. When the Lord gives someone up to a hard heart, it is one of the greatest judgments they can experience in this life. Just as God hardened Pharaoh's heart to manifest His wrath, so it is written in John 12:40: "He has blinded their eyes and hardened their hearts, so that they should not see with their eyes nor understand with their hearts, and turn, and I should heal them." Isaiah spoke these words when he saw the glory of Christ. This passage from Isaiah 6 is quoted multiple times in the Gospel as a severe judgment of God upon sinners. It is a terrible affliction to suffer from kidney or bladder stones, with the agonizing pain it causes. However, having a stone in the heart is even worse than having a stone in the bladder. If you were acquainted with the things of God, you would regard it as a greater misery. Even if you had the pain of bladder stones, you would rejoice and thank God for it if it could soften your heart. But the hardness of heart, this stony condition, is the most dreadful judgment of God that can befall a person in this world, apart from being immediately condemned to hell. In fact, it may prove to be an even greater judgment, as it accumulates wrath against the day of judgment. This leads us to the third aspect of the evil of a hard heart: those with hardened hearts throughout their lives are only storing up wrath for the day of judgment (Romans 2:4). The men and women who live in the world with hardened hearts are constantly treasuring up wrath for the day of judgment. How dreadful their condition will be in the end!

Those with hardened hearts are not affected by the Word of God or the ordinances of God. Whatever they hear, whatever is revealed to them, all the heart-melting mercies of God in the Gospel, and all the heart-breaking truths that expose the evil of sin, serve no good purpose for them. Instead, these things only increase their sin and condemnation if they persist in their hardness of heart. It is a sorrowful state for a person to be in, where all the heart-breaking mercies of God in Christ and the heart-breaking truths revealed in the Word, meant to bring about so much good for some, become aggravations of my sin and condemnation. The text tells us that those who witnessed the miracles of Christ in Matthew 6:52 did not consider them or let them affect them due to the hardness of their hearts. Nothing can penetrate a hard heart. You may think that if Christ were alive again and performing miracles before our eyes, our hearts would be moved. But if you had been alive among those Jews and witnessed Christ and His miracles, they would not have impacted you if you had a hard heart. Therefore, a hard heart resists all means of grace.

A hardened heart prepares itself for any kind of sin, it is ready for any sin. If you are kept from committing a sin, it is only because you have not encountered the right temptation. It is not out of fear of God that you abstain from it. If your heart is hard, you are susceptible to all temptations and the grossest sins in the world. This is evident in Ephesians 4:19, where it is said of those who have given themselves over to lasciviousness, working all uncleanness with greediness, that they are "past feeling." It implies that they would not be so eager in pursuing their lusts if they were not numb to moral sensibilities. When a person becomes "past feeling," they quickly fall into lasciviousness, engaging in impure acts with great eagerness. This happens because they have lost their ability to feel and discern the wrongfulness of their actions. Moreover, when individuals persist in committing great sins, it is a clear indication that they are past feeling. Those who continue in wanton and unclean behaviour are demonstrating that they have lost sensitivity to moral values.

Another consequence of a hard heart is that it paves the way for great misery, afflictions, and judgments. Whoever you are, if you have a hard heart, you are on the verge of committing some vile sin or facing a fearful judgment. It may even be that you are on the brink of both. This is stated in Proverbs 29:1 and 28:14. "Happy is the man who always fears, but he who hardens his heart will fall into trouble." In Proverbs 29:1, it is said, "He who is often reproved, yet stiffens his neck, will suddenly be broken beyond healing." When your heart resists God's Word and the admonitions of your conscience and those who warn you, you are hardening yourself against them. Oh, tremble before the Lord, for He declares that you will be suddenly destroyed, and there will be no remedy.

Furthermore, know that the Lord has sworn the destruction of a hard-hearted sinner. In Hebrews 3:8, it says, "Do not harden your hearts as in the rebellion, on the day of testing in the wilderness." The apostle strongly exhorts against the hardening of hearts. Then in verse 11, he continues, "As I swore in my wrath, 'They shall not enter my rest.'" The Lord swears against a person with a hard heart. The Lord has sworn your destruction if your heart remains hardened. You are in such a condition that, as far as you know, your ruin and destruction have been sworn by the Lord. Therefore, be cautious about persisting in the hardness of your heart for too long, lest God's oath is specifically directed against you.

Furthermore, understand that when the time of your destruction comes, if your heart is hard, the heart of God will be hardened against you when you come under His stroke. Just as the Lord deals frowardly with those who walk in wickedness, according to Scripture, His heart is hardened against a hard heart.

Even though God calls you through His Word and reveals truths that could melt the heart of a devil, your heart remains hardened. When God warns you to beware of certain sins, your heart is hardened. Is your heart hardened when you encounter the Word of God? It would be the same with the Lord if, in your most severe affliction, you cry out to Him for mercy, and He hardens His heart against you. Indeed, He threatens to respond in kind to those who harden themselves against Him. In Ezekiel 7:12, it is said, "They made their hearts as hard as stone." And verse 13 states, "Therefore it shall be, that when they cry out to me, I will not listen to them; so they shall cry out to me, but I will not listen to them, says the Lord God." When people harden their hearts against God, He, in righteous judgment, hardens His heart against them when He comes in His wrath. We find a fitting scripture in the Book of Lamentations 3:65, which says, "Give them sorrow of heart, your curse to them." The phrase translated as "sorrow of heart" can also mean a covering of the heart. Arias Montanus translates it as "give them a covering of heart." Commentators on the passage explain that this word sometimes signifies a disease in the body, a condition where there is a hard film around the heart that covers it, preventing any kind of comfort or nourishment from reaching it. Give them such a heart condition, and your curse with it. Those who have hardness of heart that prevents God's commands and truths from penetrating them, it is just for God to give them such a covering on their hearts in times of affliction that no comfort can reach them. In your health and prosperity, you hear these truths that God expects your hearts to be moved and sensitive to, yet they do not touch you. Well, when you face affliction, the Lord may send a curse that creates a hardness around your heart, so that whatever is said to comfort you will never reach your heart. Just as now, whatever is said to bring about your contrition does not touch your heart. And is this not just? Oh, it would be a dreadful curse from God if it were so!

You know further that God has a time to make people aware, despite their hardened hearts. In one way or another, their hearts will be brought to some kind of tenderness, so they may feel the evil of sin and realize the greatness of the God they have to deal with. There are two types of tenderness:

1. Tenderness that arises from having the right disposition of the flesh.

2. Tenderness that arises from the afflictions of the flesh.

The saints of God have a sensitivity, but their sensitivity is the result of having the right disposition of their hearts, and it does not harm them. They are sensitive to God's threats and promises, and there is joy in their sensitivity. However, for wicked individuals who are currently insensitive, the Lord has a time when He will make them sensitive. The Lord will bring affliction upon their hearts, and then they will become sensitive. In Ezekiel 21:7, it is written, "And it shall be when they say to you, 'Why are you sighing?' that you shall answer, 'Because of the news; when it comes, every heart will melt, all hands will be feeble, every spirit will faint, and all knees will be weak as water. Behold, it is coming and shall be brought to pass,' says the Lord God." Every heart shall melt. In this passage, we have an example of a gracious, melting heart that God accepts. However, if your hearts do not melt when you hear the Word, God will melt your hearts in the future through dreadful news of fearful judgments. Thus, it is stated in Jeremiah 9:7-8, "Therefore thus says the Lord of hosts: 'Behold, I will refine them and test them, for how shall I deal with the daughter of my people? Their tongue is an arrow shot out; it speaks deceit; one speaks peaceably to his neighbor with his mouth, but in his heart he lies in wait. Shall I not punish them for these things?' says the Lord. 'Shall I not avenge Myself on such a nation as this?'" So, if your hearts do not melt when you hear the Word, the Lord has a time, in spite of your hardened hearts, to melt you. Therefore, to conclude, in illustrating the evil of a hard heart, I refer to Job 9:5: "Who has hardened his heart against Him and prospered?" So I say to every man or woman with a hard heart, who has hardened their heart against the Lord and prospered? You may continue to please yourself in your own ways and believe that you will have your will and do as you please. Let them say what they can, but know that no one who has hardened their heart against the Lord has prospered. What has become of all the hard-hearted sinners who have lived in the past? Show me one example of a person who has hardened their heart against the Lord and prospered. The end for them is ruin, misery, and eternal destruction.

But you might say, "I hope we do not have hard hearts. We acknowledge that having a heart hardened against the Lord is a fearful judgment."

No, are your hearts not hardened against the Lord? Then how is it that you are so complacent in your sins? Certainly, a person who can be so calm in known sin has a hard heart. You are conscious of the sins you live in, and yet you can eat, drink, socialize, and be merry. Oh, you hard-hearted sinner, hardened in your sins! If your heart were tender, even if you had fallen into sin (as we all do, that must be acknowledged), it would trouble you like a mote in your eye. There may be much dirt on your hand that doesn't bother you, but a small mote in your eye would greatly trouble you.

Furthermore, men have hard hearts, otherwise the Word of God and the works of God would win their hearts for the Lord, but they do not. We see today that the blessed truths of God, which are revealed more clearly and fully than ever before, hardly touch the hearts of many. Even the great works of God, where He appears most glorious, fail to captivate the hearts of men. Surely, their hearts are very hard.

Indeed, men's hearts are hard because their hearts are proud. A proud heart is always a hard heart. The more pride there is, the more hardness resides in the heart. As it is written in Daniel 5:20, "But when his heart was lifted up, and his mind hardened in pride..." Proud and obstinate individuals, those who are determined in their ways and are proud and stubborn, they are people with hard hearts.

Again, surely the hearts of men are exceedingly hard. It is evident in the fact that they can easily come into God's presence, confess their sins before Him, and judge themselves worthy of destruction because of their sins. Yet, they can leave and continue living in their sins despite all of this. This displays a dreadful hardness of heart, and it is distressingly common in our time. We have many days of fasting and prayer, where we come before God and narrate our sins to Him, making detailed confessions. We judge ourselves for our sins. However, after all of this, how many sins are truly amended? Let any family come forward and say, "O Lord, since those fasting days, we have confessed these particular sins, judged ourselves for them, and by Your grace, they have been corrected." I fear that only a few souls would be able to honestly make such a statement in the presence of God. Certainly, on the day of fasting, you either do this or you do not. If the minister addresses your specific sins, you join in agreement and say, "Amen" to their confessions. If the minister does not mention your particular sins, then, if you truly desire to sanctify a fast to God as you should, you will find a private place and confess those sins that were not confessed publicly. I appeal to you on behalf of the Lord: Have you observed such fasts? Have you paid attention to whether the minister addressed your individual sins or not? And if they did not, have you gone alone and examined your hearts privately, acknowledging the sins you are guilty of? Have you judged yourselves for them but failed to reform? Certainly, if you have not done this, you have not truly understood what it means to observe a fast. And if you have done this yet continue in the same sins, it indicates a terrifying hardness of heart. How can we come into God's presence, confess our sins openly, and yet not wholeheartedly strive against them? Truly, our hearts are greatly hardened before the Lord.

Furthermore, it is worth noting that God's mercy itself can harden people. The more individuals experience the shine of God's mercy, the more they become hardened in their sins. There are many who, during times of affliction, appear to be vulnerable and pliable like iron. However, once their afflictions subside, they return to their former hardness. Their hearts are akin to clay, which hardens under the beams of the sun.

Indeed, it is a clear indication that we possess hard hearts when we show little sensitivity towards the sufferings of our brethren in other parts of the world. They cry out to us for help, and we hear their sorrowful complaints and pleas. They are stripped of their possessions, their wives violated before their very eyes, and they are left with nothing. Yet, we lack mercy and compassion towards them. Because our own tables are filled, and we live in comfort and ease, we fail to take to heart the afflictions of our brethren and the broader calamities befalling the Church. I dare to appeal to this entire congregation and to each individual soul present: How deeply have you internalised the current state of the Church and its collective struggles? Do these matters truly touch your heart? Can you find a solitary place and lament with a sorrowful spirit? Does your heart melt and dissolve into tears when you hear of the sufferings of your brethren and the overall calamities facing the Church? But if these things do not affect you, and you remain unaffected and merry, continuing to follow the ways of the world, it is clear that you are a person with a hard heart. Therefore, tremble before the Lord.

And for those of you who are in such a state, all the comforting words spoken about having a tender heart in the previous discussion may not apply to you, and it is concerning that you may have no share or part in that experience.

However, some of you might say, "I thank God that my heart is not so hard. I do feel a sensitivity in my heart towards these things."

Indeed, but this sensitivity may fall short of the spiritual sensitivity that was present in Josiah. Therefore, the next point of examination should be whether our hearts are tender in a spiritual sense, which is the work of the Holy Spirit sanctifying our hearts.

First of all, we need to understand that there can be a softness of heart that arises from one's natural disposition.

Secondly, there can be temporary emotional responses in the heart upon hearing the Word.

And thirdly, there can be a sense of fear and conviction in the heart through knowledge of the Law.

Regarding the first point, a plum or cherry may appear soft on the outside but be hard inside.

Similarly, as for the second point, we know that ice can thaw during the day and freeze again at night.

And concerning the terrors of the Law, we are aware that a marble stone may seem to melt and trickle down with tears in wet weather, but it remains a stone nonetheless.

www.ingramcontent.com/pod-product-compliance
Lightning Source LLC
Chambersburg PA
CBHW040555010526
44110CB00055B/2785